A RIVER TO CROSS

A DOCUMENTED ACCOUNT

JOHN HOWARD McCLELLAN
2010

An historical account showing by narrative, detailed maps and illustrations of the actual locations that General Robert E. Lee and his Confederate Army bivouacked and headquartered on their way to Virginia after the Battle of Gettysburg; including a brief account of The Battle of Monterey Pass, Monterey Springs, Pennsylvania.

Permission granted for use of photo on cover by
National Baseball Hall of Fame Library
Cooperstown, N.Y.

Library of Congress Cataloging-in-Publication Data
John Howard McClellan 1927-
A River to Cross by John Howard McClellan
includes maps, illustrations, bibliographical reference & testimonials

1st Printing

ISBN 978-0-9790983-4-5

Manufactured in the United States of America

Copyquik Printing and Graphics, LLC
710 Oak Hill Avenue, Hagerstown, MD. 21740
www.copyquik.com

10 9 8 7 6 5 4 3 2

OLD STONE HOUSE

CHARMIAN, PA.

Benchoof Homestead

A pen and ink sketch from the 1920's of the John Benchoof Homestead on the Furnace Road showing Lee's Rock #1, by Mary K. Porter, a Washington, D.C. artist.

Dedication

To Terry Lee McClellan
without whose love and loyalty there would
have been no book

Acknowledgements

When we begin to acknowledge the help and assistance we have received in so many ways in the research and writing of even a small volume of local history with a subject as obscure as this volume and which was written over a period of time that it has consumed; it gives us pause to be able to say exactly when it was begun and exactly who it is we want to thank for their help and support, the spectrum becomes so broad and time tends to dim the memory of those many individuals that rendered their assistance in so many subtle ways.

In offering our sincere thanks, there are bound to be those that are overlooked. The best we can do is advance our acknowledgements for their help and assure those we've overlooked that our omissions are not intentional and our thanks to them are justly sincere.

To those who helped us on numerous occasions and in various ways, all we can say is our heartfelt thanks to all.

Ted Alexander, the late Clarence Barnard, the late Mary B. Barton, Francis L. Benchoff, the late John Krebs Benchoff, the late Lucy Foust Benchoff, Mrs. Nancy Bert, Theodore A. Black, the late Harvey Bridgers, David E. Cline, the late Greg Coco, Charles Fennell, the late Melb Foreman, Dennis E. Frye, John C. Frye, the late Charles Gardner, Sr., the late Charles S. Gardner, Jr., Ruth Baer Gembe, Charles H. Glatfelter, Letitia G. Gardner, Deborah W. Knauer, Mike Marshall, Barry D. Martin, Nicole Bissonette Martin, Christy Jo McClellan, Richard E. McClellan, Robert M. McClellan, Thomas K. McClellan, Kathleen O'Connell, the late Anne Marie Reed, Richard A. & Judy Rice, the late Homer T. Rosenberger, the late Hazel Adams Schaeffer, the late C. Omar Tracey, R. J. Ternes, the late C. Anderson Warner, the late Robert Watson

Table Of Contents

FOREWORD

This book is a chronicle of the whereabouts of Robert E. Lee and his Army of Northern Virginia after the Battle of Gettysburg, up to the time they withdrew across the Potomac River on their journey back to their native Southern soil. It is not the purpose of this volume to simply add to the verbiage that has been published over the years about Gettysburg and the famous battle. Its intent is to document an obscure and overlooked part of the history of the post-Gettysburg battle and to pinpoint the locations of certain retreat landmarks and occurrences. There has been a great deal written on the chronology of troop movements, units and their leaders, both of the Union and of the Confederate. Who pursued whom, which units advanced and which retreated, locations of skirmishes, of both armies, but little has been accurately written on what happened locally in the wake of the fighting and how those closest to the conflict were affected. In research, we found that one figure was paramount not only to the battle, but to its aftermath and to the people of the Confederacy and the citizens of the United States. As he was prominent, while living, so is he still, although he has been gone these many years. He was General Robert E. Lee.

You will find this work documented by word of mouth, legend and written record and there will be some (a lot of) controversy about that which has been written. Many readers, experts and amateurs, will find some of the opinions set forth uncomplimentary to both the Union and the Confederacy, they are not meant to be. You may find this work sacrilegious to the accepted reverence henceforth afforded the sacred memories of the respected commanders of both forces. There will be different views concerning their personalities, their abilities, their appearances and their whereabouts.

When we were young, there were still residents of Gettysburg and vicinity, albeit old men and women, that were still of sound memory of the battle that took place in their youth. At home, at the store, at school, at church there were often conversations about what they or their parents remembered and had said. Sometimes these people were anxious to point out certain sites and incidents as happening contrary to the accepted newspaper or published accounts of the day. We tried to fully attend to what they said, although the full importance of what they said did not become apparent until many long years after they had said it and we regret that we did not pay closer attention to what was repeatedly said to try to impress it on our young mind. When we were boys, it was just a battle to us.

Some accounts in this volume are based on the narration of family tradition. These, for the most part, but not always, relate to artifacts and heirlooms. They sometimes relate to sites and incidents. Much of what follows is based on early writings that are rare, if not, obscure in nature and necessitated lengthy and painstaking research into archival manuscript sources, including soldier's diaries, letters and memoirs in handwritten form. It seems that more and more material of this type is becoming available as time elapses. The value of this material has become increasingly evident to the individuals who have held or withheld it from the public domain. Through education, the Internet, and the broadening of knowledge and understanding of the historical importance of events including wars, this material once enviably treasured and closely held, is now being more freely shared. This is a good thing and a responsible act on the part of individuals. Some of this material has been found to be sentimental and sub-jective. Some of it comes from memoirs and histories written many years after the Battle of Gettysburg and should be weighed as such.

It is impossible to define the intense interest displayed by the hundreds of thousands of people that are drawn to this civil war among Americans, mainly because their purposes are so diverse. There are the hero worshippers, the plain and pure history buffs, genealogists, the hobbyists and actors or should we say, re-enactors, the strategians and war gamers, the Union and Confederate sympathizers, the soldier and ancestor worshippers of both federations, the collectors of books on the subject, collectors of artifacts and weapons, of photos, of clothing, buttons, money, stamps and insignia and of those categories fall into a myriad of combinations of one or more of the above.

It still astonishes me, beyond belief; that there is so much interest in a cruel war in which so many gave their lives in a dispute over two such derogatory causes. One cause being whether one man has the right to enslave another, a "duh" principle that the majority of citizens of the United States had resisted in the past, revolted against and formed a new nation based on the principles contrary to the bondage of one man or one woman to another. It is my fervent hope that we will continue to oppose any such principle. The second cause being whether the citizens of one state of the United States has the right to recant its allegiance to those States United and, in effect, form a separate country within that country. If for no other reason, the outcome of The War of the Rebellion seems to have settled the latter question for the balance of time. There is no guarantee of this, however, the principle of civil disobedience still has its advocates, in the United States, even in modern times the fomenting dissension within our country, since the turn of the 21st century still continues to influence important events.

I hope that my years of research will have produced a work, while not in the strictest sense a history, one worthy of interest to readers of all ages as a chronicle not only when it happened but where it happened, during those difficult days not only for the general populous, but for particularly Lee and his soldiers, and that it will provide insight into a complicated and long overlooked aspect of the era following the Battle of Gettysburg.

CHAPTER ONE

A Sunday Morning German

The old lady never knew what made her step down from the porch that morning, but, as she did, she looked up with a start. There in the lane, were a group of mounted soldiers dressed in all manner of clothing; gray, butternut brown, even red uniforms. There was a greater array of headgear: gray, brown and black. Some of the men wore hats with plumes, some were bareheaded, some wore floppy hats, some wore tall and some wore slouch hats. There were uniforms with gold braid and insignia. Some were plain. She was sure they were Confederates and that the war had finally come to her home. She had no way to know that this army was in full retreat. She cried out to them, more out of fear than friendliness. They had halted near the bank barn. She was afraid that, as the enemy, they would set it on fire.

"Come on ahead and have some tea and biscuits. You are welcome." She was even more certain that they were Confederate when she saw them recoil slightly. They were caught unaware. They were not used to such civility from Unionists. Union women were usually dour looking women, frowning or scowling. She well knew the uniform of a Union soldier. After all, her son was the Provost Marshal of the Pennsylvania Militia in the county in which they lived. It was his duty to preserve military order, govern the military police, capture deserters and recover stolen government property.

William F. Benchoof (1826-1896) was a farmer, entrepreneur,

Benchoof Homstead Ca 1990

The Benchoff home as it looked in the 1990's This house was built about by immigrant John Benchoff and witnessed General Kilpatrick's charge through the Monterey Pass and General Robert E. Lee's impromptu tea party with the local ladies. Montana Springs Hotel stood to the right center in photo.

land developer and hotelkeeper, keeping the Montana Springs Hotel on this same farm. During the Civil War he served as Provost Marshal for the 126th Regiment of the Pennsylvania Volunteer Infantry organized at Chambersburg, Franklin County, Pennsylvania. His father was John Benchoof (1790-1874), a native of Germany. The modern spelling of this family name is now Benchoff, but there are still many variations of it i.e. Banzhof, Benshoff, etc.[1]

The soldiers advanced slowly and as they drew closer she could see that they were in a state of fatigue. Their uniforms were sodden and muddy with a curious smoky hue. So much so, that it was difficult to distinguish either stripes, stars or bars!

Granny[2] and some of the ladies of the neighborhood were having a Sunday morning german[3], but with all the talk being about the previous night's skirmishing and commotion right in

---

1 See: U.S. Census on Microfilm, Washington Twp. Franklin County, PA. Post Office-Waynesboro, 4 July 1860, pp. 956-958; Also U.S. Census on Microfilm for the years 1850 and 1870, same Township & County. Also Septennial Census on Microfilm for Pennsylvania Years 1856 and 1863, Pennsylvania Historical and Museum Commission, State Archives, Harrisburg, PA. Benchoff Genealogical information from Antietam Ancestors, Volume III, No. 3, #1(cont'd) Summer Edition, 1989; Conochocheague Genealogical Society, Waynesboro, PA. 17268; Also Benchoff family tradition as related to the author by descendants.

2 *Granny* was Sarah Ann Miller. Born 1795 She was the mother of William F. Benchoof. Family stories related that her daughter-in-law, Mary Ann Crawford and the other ladies in the group were very much perturbed that the old lady would invite Rebels to tea, even after they found out they were distinguished Confederate officers.

3 A german was a gathering derived from the early cotillion dances of France and Germany, which were generally held in the morning and later evolved, in America, into piano recitals, sings, readings and recitations, whist parties, bible study and eventually Sunday schools. Refreshments were generally served and local gossip and political discussions were commonplace.

their own backyard there was little interest in the scripture, hymn singing, prayer and such and it would appear that Granny Benchoof had little choice. If she hadn't invited them to tea, they would have surely raided her hen house, pigpen and other livestock. Who was to say that they would not still do so.

By this time, the horsemen had arrived in front of the house and the other ladies were by Granny's side. There was no mistaking the eldest officer on the iron gray horse.[4] It was undoubtedly General Robert E. Lee. His uniform was well worn but not shoddy. He looked extremely dignified, neat and clean compared to his companions. After he had dismounted, he raised his hat as a greeting of respect to all the ladies and they crowded around him in a small circle. As an introduction, he said, "General Lee, Army of Northern Virginia. May I present General Longstreet and members of our staff?" The ladies were awestruck. When they regained their composure, they smiled, bowed and curtsied

---

4   The iron gray horse was, of course, Traveller, a handsome stallion with black points, his mane and tail being very dark. He was sixteen hands high and was six years old at this time. He had a bold carriage and great muscular strength. He was a sensible horse, afraid of nothing. Yet, if not exercised regularly or given a "breather" as General Lee had been heard to say, he became fretful and chafed at restraint especially in the company of other horses. If he was ridden, regularly and hard, after a good gallop, he would proceed at a quiet walk, however, many, even Robert E. Lee, would not have called this gait a walk and they were not so fond of its jarring motion. Lee did admit in his latter years at Lexington, shortly before his death, in a letter to his son, Fitzhugh, 2 December 1869, "the present weather, I hope will be beneficial, enabling me to ride and be in the open air. But, Traveller's trot is harder to me than it used to be and fatigues me." See Lee Recollections and Letters, p. 267. *For more on Traveller see Appendix at the end of text...*

8

and called for tea for the visitors. "Bring the big teapot."[5] someone called. The teapot and cups were there in an instant along with cake and cookies, jam, biscuits, bread and butter; the ladies probably held back the fresh baked cherry pie. There was no shortage of these victuals

Photo courtesy of the late John Krebs Benchoff

The Lee Tea Pot

Benchoff Family heirloom the "big" teapot that served General Lee and his staff.

in the North particularly in Pennsylvania and further to the North. Trade was carried on there as if there was no war in progress and the further you proceeded into New York and New England the more normal life became.

The horses drank at the spring by the large stone.[6] The officers feasted on handfuls of pastry and drank the tea, which

---

5   The big teapot illustrated is a Benchoff family heirloom and the tradition of Lee and his staff being served from it has been perpetuated through the generations. It is an eight cup teapot of soft cream paste ware, Sunderland in appearance but unmarked, except for an incised "8" in its base. It is 12 inches from spout to handle, 6 inches wide and 6 inches high, 8 inches high to the finial of the lid. Its glaze is crazed as well as heat discolored. It has a painted pattern of dark blue flowers with a dark red center, reminiscent of the *Sprig* pattern. (Related by Lucy Chambers Foust Benchoff, Mrs. Walter B. Benchoff, Mrs. James M. Benchoff and Harriett Benchoff Ritchey.)

6   The large boulder in the photo of the John Benchoof homestead shown here is one of two legendary Lee's Rocks' in this locale. This one is reputed to be the rock upon which Lee sat and drank his tea in company with the ladies while his staff watered the horses and enjoyed their tea and biscuits. The *second* Lee's Rock is claimed to be further along Lee's route of the retreat. A photo and description of Lee's Rock #2 appears on page #98. (The location of Lee's Rock #1 was related by Hazel Schaeffer, Roy Benchoff and Francis L. Benchoff.)

they laced heavily with fresh cream and sugar. This was the first good fare that any of them had in at least twenty-four hours. What then took place was the classic scenario of Lee and the ladies, an oft-repeated interlude throughout the life of General Lee. As a young man, "He went much in the society of the ladies – always most congenial to him. His conversation was bright, his wit refined and pleasant. Cement mortar, lime, curves, tangents and straight professional lines disappeared then. He enjoyed a dress parade of this (the female) kind, was as happy in the drawing room in the evening and as (he was) happy in his work on the next day."[7]

The outward appearance of General Lee was one thing, but, his personal magnetism was another, "Those who have never known him cannot imagine the charm of his manner, the brightness of his smile and the pleasant way he had of speaking, especially to young people and little children. His rebukes to the young were administered in the kindest, gentlest way, almost persuasively, but, he could be stern when occasion demanded."[8]

That he was a "ladies man" is further admitted: "Among the company (this was at White Sulphur Springs in Baltimore Row. In company with W.W. Corcoran, Washington, D.C.; Prof. J&J. White of Washington and Lee; Miss Mary Pendleton; Agnes Fitzhugh and others during the stay of August, 1867.) were many old friends and acquaintances from Baltimore who could not suffi-

---

7   Lee, Fitzhugh, (nephew), <u>General Lee</u>, Appleton Century Co. Inc, New York, 1895, p.25
8   Lee, Robert E. Capt, (son) <u>Recollections and Letters of General Robert E. Lee</u>, New York, Doubleday, 1904, p.315

ciently testify to their pleasure in the renewal of this intercourse. Whenever he appeared in the parlour or ballroom he was the center of attraction and, in vain, the young men tried to engage the attention of the young ladies whenever General Lee was present."

During the Valley Campaign "General Lee would often leave the front, come into Richmond and attend the parties and on such occasion he was not only the cynosure of all eyes, but the ladies all crowded around him and he kissed everyone of them and he seemed to enjoy the exercise of it. On such occasions he was thoroughly urbane but was always the dignified patrician soldier in his bearing."[9]

An aide-de-camp of General Ewell paints a vivid word picture of General Lee when they met at the Battle of Gettysburg. "General Lee received me in his grave and kindly way. He was 56 years old, of superb physique, standing 5 feet, 11 inches and one-half inches in height and weighed 175 pounds and appeared to be in perfect health. He wore a grey felt, medium brim hat. His boots fitted well, coming to his knee with a border of fair (light colored) leather. He was himself a soldier, lived as a soldier, in a tent and on the plainest fare. He neither knew tobacco nor cared for wine...He has an unruffled calm about his countenance which betokened the concentration and control of the whole being within. He was kingly man whom, when all who came within his presence, expected to obey." He further stated, "In the religion of Robert E. Lee there was faith without fanaticism, prayer without

---

9   Southern Historical Society Papers, hereafter SHSP, Volume 19, p. 382-3.

pretension, a reality, a gentleness, a simplicity that kept him brave in peril and tranquil in disaster. He feared God and was strong. He loved God and little children."[10] There are many, many such detailed descriptions of Lee. One such by Col. A. J. L. Fremantle, an officer in the British Army and an observer for the British, who traveled throughout the Confederate states for three months and was with General Longstreet's staff at the Battle of Gettysburg. The British were particularly interested in knowing whether the Confederate States were worthy of their financial support. They most readily wanted to know who was going to win this conflict. Never let it be said that the English were not smart enough to always hedge their bets. They were interested in which contestant would control future commerce.

Fremantle wrote, "General Lee is almost without exception, the handsomest man of his age I ever saw. He is fifty-six years old, tall, broad shouldered, very well made, well set-up, a thorough soldier in appearance and his manner most courteous and full of dignity. He is a perfect gentleman in every respect. I imagine no man has so few enemies or is so universally esteemed. Throughout the South all agree in pronouncing him to be as near perfect as a man can be. He has none of the small vices such as smoking, drinking, chewing or swearing and his bitterest enemy never accused him of any greater ones. He generally wears a well-worn gray jacket and a high, black felt hat and blue trousers

---

10 Petersburg, Chancellorsville and Gettysburg, no author, Military Historical Society of Massachusetts, Boston, 1906

tucked into his Wellington boots. I never saw him carry arms. [11] (Lee and Longstreet did not carry arms – General A.P. Hill generally wears a sword.) and the only mark of his rank are the three stars on his collar. He rides a handsome horse that is extremely well groomed. He, himself, is very neat in his dress and person and in the most arduous marches he always looks smart and clean." (Fremantle observed this fact during and after the three days of fighting at Gettysburg and during the muddy retreat when everyone else, officers and private soldiers looked and were extremely dirty.) A first-hand observation comes from a soldier that served in the 34th North Carolina Volunteers, "The retreat from Gettysburg cannot be described. The soldiers were so completely covered with mud, that the color of their clothing could not be distinguished."[12]

Fremantle continues, "I believe he has never slept in a house since he has commanded the Virginian army and he invariably declines all offers of hospitality for fear that the person offering it may afterwards get into trouble for having sheltered the rebel General. The relations between him and Longstreet are quite touching–they are almost always together. "Longstreet's corps complain of this sometimes … it is impossible to please Longstreet more than by praising Lee…"[13] For an apt description of his

---

11 Fitzhugh Lee, his nephew, relates " He (Gen. Lee) always carried a pistol in the holster on the left of his saddle because it was more convenient to reach when dismounted and ammunition in the right holster. This pistol hung over his bedpost in Lexington after the war and was discharged after his death not a barrel missing fire. Lee, Fitzhugh General Lee, D. Appleton & Co, N.Y., 1894.

12 Fremantle, Col. A. J. L.., Three Months in the Confederate States, William Blackwood and Son, Edinburgh and London, 1863 p. 253.

13 13 Gettysburg National Military Park, Vertical File, #7-CS-9, Vol. # 2, pp. 586-7.

power over his officers one need look no further than this: "Some of the fiercest and most inflexible men the world has ever seen were (officers) in the Army of Northern Virginia, Stonewall Jackson, Jubal A. Early, John B. Gordon, J.E.B. Stuart and John B. Hood, they would stand erect in any presence on earth, yet, they all uncovered (removed their hats) in Lee's presence.[14]

In the full twenty-four hours since the order for withdrawal was given at 1 a.m. July 4th,[15] these men had spent time arranging for two trains of withdrawal. General Imboden's troops and horses, which had been held in reserve, were fresh and were assigned to conduct a great wagon train of wounded via Cashtown, Greenwood, Marion, Greencastle and Hagerstown to

Permission of South Carolina Confederate Relic Room, Columbia, SC

Fairfield Gap

View after Dr. Simon Baruch of Jack's Mt. & Fairfield Gap from the top of Herr's Ridge on the Fairfield Road. The Blackhorse Tavern roof and barn are visible center of photo.

---

14 Fremantle, Col A.J.L. ibid, p. 253.

15 Royall, William Capt., <u>Some Reminiscenses</u>, Neale Publishing, N.Y., 1909 p. 274.

cross the Potomac at Williamsport. General Longstreet's Corps and the balance of the Army, along with the walking wounded and supply wagons, were to withdraw through Fairfield either by the Hagerstown Turnpike, now known as the Jack's Mountain Road or by the Maria Furnace Road through the Monterey Gap, toward Leitersburg and Hagerstown. They were then to continue to the same river crossing where more than a fortnight ago, they had crossed by ford and pontoon bridge into enemy territory. General Stuart's cavalry was to protect the left flank of both trains and guard prisoners by proceeding to Thurmont, then known as Mechanicstown, thence along the eastern side of the mountains to Smithsburg, by Hagerstown to Williamsport, keeping themselves between the Union Army and the retiring Confederates.

Permission of Adams Co. Historical Society, Gettysburg, PA

Blackhorse Tavern

An 1880's view of the Blackhorse Tavern (Bream's) that served as a Confederate field hospital and as shelter and respite for Confederate soldiers after the Battle of Gettysburg.

Darkness on the 4th found Lee and Longstreet at Breams Hill near the Blackhorse Tavern on the Fairfield Road observing the marching troops and passing train and later in a field along this same road near the Lower Marsh Creek Church.[16] Later, Lee and his staff spent a soggy night in camp along Tom's Creek near the intersection of the Old Furnace and the Maria Furnace Road.[17]

Maria Furnace was owned by that nemesis of slavery and ardent abolitionist, Thaddeus Stevens.[18] It had conveniently been destroyed by fire many years before. The furnace had never done well financially. It is probably safe to say that had it not already been burned, the Confederates with no love lost for Stevens, would have surely put it to the torch just as General Jubal A. Early

---

16 General John B. Imboden relates that he was summoned to meet with General Lee at 11:00 p.m. on July 3rd and was directed to wait for him at his headquarters, which he did, but Lee did not appear until 1:00 a.m. on the 4th of July. Imboden was directed to organize and have his troops conduct a wagon train of wounded back to Virginia. This was no simple task and a dangerous mission, too, because he had neither the men nor the means (food, supplies or ammunition) to do so. Both Lee and Imboden expected the 15 to 17 mile long wagon train would be subjected to considerable harassment by Union scouts and cavalry. This proved not to be the case, the most damage to this train was done at Greencastle, Franklin County by a group of civilians, who fell upon the train *en masse* with axes and saws, hammers, picks and mattocks and cut the wheel spokes on the wheels of about one dozen wagons. (Battles and Leaders of the Civil War, Volume 3, p. 420.)

17 "When it was dusk, we went a mile or two farther on the Fairfield Road (*from the tavern at Bream's*) and presently came upon a blazing fire around which were Generals Lee and Longstreet with all their staff. We were to remain here until the train had passed, when the main body of the army would be withdrawn from its position and join the retreat." (Ross Fitzgerald, A Visit to the Cities and Camps of the Confederate States; Richard B Harwell, Editor, Reprint Edition, University of Illinois Press, 1958 p. 54.

18 This location was traditional among local residents, Robert W. Watson, Roy Benchoff and J. Melbourn Foreman, all of who were native to the area. Fremantle states that he came upon General Lee early on the morning of July 5th, seated at a table beside a picturesque little stream. (Blackwood's Magazine, Edinburgh, 1866)

had burned Stevens' Caledonia Furnace at the beginning of the Pennsylvania invasion.[19]

Courtesy of the Hamiltonban Township, Adams County Historical Society

Maria Furnace Ruins

The last remnants of the manor house Maria Furnace, Iron Springs, Adams County, PA.

---

19 Thaddeus Stevens (1792-1868) was a former resident of Gettysburg and Adams County, but left there in 1842, among scandals and financial reversals, to reside in Lancaster. He was powerful State and United States political leader. He was one of the founders and saviors of the free public educational system as we know it today and a vigorous proponent of the abolition of slavery, supposedly involved in the *Underground Railroad* and the author of the 13th Amendment to the Constitution of the United States. He was persuasive speaker and not only supported abolition but also strongly supported other citizenship and voters rights reform. He had built Maria Furnace in partnership with James Paxson in 1830. This Furnace was never financially successful. He was also the builder of the Gettysburg to Hagerstown Railroad (*The Tapeworm Railroad*), which became defunct after spending $700.000 in state grant money, which Stevens had obtained through his political influence as Chairman of the Pennsylvania House Ways and Means Committee. (Article-Gettysburg Times, 5 December 1897 and Pamphlet-Thaddeus Stevens, Published John Hancock Life Insurance Co. np, nd.)

17

The Maria Furnace Road, sometimes called the Old Furnace Road, now called the Gum Springs Road on the Adams County side of the county line, and the Furnace Road in Franklin County, had brought General Lee and his retinue to the Benchoof farm. These officers had been traveling the Maria Furnace Road along with the troops and in the wake of General Early's wagon train that had left it so deep in mud and mire that horses could barely travel.[20] This so impeded their progress that they decided to take a by-road that turned east in the vicinity of the Gum Spring. This by-road was actually a Benchoof farm lane that brought them to tea and biscuits with the ladies. While they refreshed themselves and their mounts were grazing, a dispatch rider galloped up and dismounted. He presented General Lee with a message. How he had found these officers, so far from the beaten track was not known, suffice it to say that it was the business of the common soldier to be privy to a grapevine of information and to know the whereabouts of their leaders at all times.

Century Illustrated Monthly Magazine

Courier

Looking to deliver a dispatch.

20 This route of retreat through Fairfield and the Monterey Gap has been many times described. Fremantle wrote, "5th July (Sunday)—The night was very bad—thunder and lightning, torrents of rain—the road knee deep in mud and water and often

Footnote #20 (Cont'd)

blocked up with wagons 'come to grief.' I pitied the wretched plight of the unfortunate soldiers who were to follow us. Our progress was naturally very slow indeed, and we took eight hours to go as many miles."(Fremantle, op.cit. p. 221. The plight of the foot soldier was one thing, but the conditions for others, such as the teamsters, the drovers and the animals was another. The road was so blocked up with wagons, ambulances, artillery pieces, caissons, horses, cattle, cavalry, marching men, walking wounded, that progress was well nigh impossible. "Army teamsters were never appreciated at their true value by soldiers in the field, for it was the general opinion that 'any fool can drive mules'. Those who tried the experiment found the teamsters office not a sinecure. The successful handling of six stubborn, pugnacious brutes required a degree of patience, skill and will power only developed by long experience. When the roads were dry and even, wagon driving was a pastime, but, when the trains reached the mountain passes or the roads became seas of mud, then the task was no joke. Mud three feet deep, as tenacious as stiff clay could make it, rendered the movement of wagons and artillery a difficult (and dangerous) operation. The wheels were solid disks of mud and the labor for both men and animals was multiplied four-fold. Then the genius of the teamster was manifested. With an inexhaustible vocabulary of oaths at (his) command and armed with a formidable snake whip, both were used with a startling and telling effect. The air, blue with profanity and the huge whip whistling cruelly on the backs of the quivering brutes, gave them new strength and the mired vehicle soon emerged from its muddy bed, (Only to sink inexorably into the next sinkhole). It was a leading article of faith among teamsters that mules could only be driven by constant cursing and they lived up to that belief with rare constancy. An attempt to drive a team of mules without cursing invariably proved a failure, because the animals had become so accustomed to that method of persuasion that they would not move without it. Teamsters as a class were brave and untiring in their peculiar sphere of duty, but they got little credit from the rank and file, being generally looked upon as men unwilling to fight. They could fight, however, for the teamsters frequently saved their trains from capture by stubborn resistance when attacked. Every wagon carried a loaded musket and the weapons were often used with deadly effect.

Many a brave mule driver died like a hero in defending the property intrusted (sic) to his charge, though there was seldom any record of such bravery.

To see an ordnance train gallop upon a battle field was an exhilarating sight, for the teamsters were then in their glory. Coming up on the wagons wheeled into line as cleverly as if the men were moving field pieces into position and the mules strained every muscle and obeyed every command with remarkable docility. (Hinman, W.F. Compiler, Camp and Field,Hamilton Publishing Co., Cleveland, 1892)

Couriers and aide-de-camps were the elite of the army, while not being commissioned officers; they were generally the favored and selected for their intelligence and their loyalty, being knowledgeable in all sorts of important information.

The General read the dispatch with care and handed it to Longstreet and in his serious way said, "It's the prisoners." With that statement, he courteously thanked the ladies for their generosity, probably bowed, started for Traveller, slowly and carefully mounted and with that small ceremony, he and his little troop were gone... almost as quickly as they had appeared.

CHAPTER TWO

The Non-Parole at Monterey

When General Lee and his little troop took leave of the Benchoof ladies, their route took them down a winding lane that passed Margaret Zeilinger's[1] farm, which was the central point of much frenzied activity during the stormy fighting of the previous night. They traveled onward to meet the Waynesboro, Greencastle and Mercersburg (WGM) Turnpike[2] that was the first surfaced road they had traversed since leaving Gettysburg over the

---

1   Margaret Zeilinger was the widow of George A. Zeilinger (b.ca.1800-1861?) a farmer and laborer, a native of Hesse-Darmstadt in Germany whose land adjoined the Benchoof's and Henry Gordon's. The widow, Margaret and his daughters, Elizabeth, Margaret and Henrietta kept the place going by operating a boarding house, hiring out as servants and growing cash crops. More on the heroism Henrietta later.
2   The Waynesburg, Greencastle and Mercersburg Turnpike (Baltimore Pike) was a well maintained road dating from its incorporation in 1816 by the Pennsylvania

Baltimore Turnpike at Fairfield. The WGM Turnpike was also known as the Baltimore Pike. Southward it climbed steeply to a summit passing Henry Gordon's field that had been occupied the night before by the Confederate artillery.[3] Moving southward as Lee and party were, this pike carried upward leading to a summit where the Monterey Springs Hotel[4] was located. This recently built resort hotel had changed possession between the Confederate and the Union Armies, at least, three times within the twenty-four hours that passed since Lee's Army had begun its withdrawal from the battlefield at Gettysburg.

At present, this hotel and its outbuildings were in the possession of the Confederacy; all residents and employees had been placed under house arrest. The place was a veritable beehive of frenzied activity and upon General Lee's arrival all roads, lanes and by-ways leading to the place were doubly picketed. Later estimates were made that from 10,000 to 20,000 troops [both

Footnote #2 (Cont'd)

Legislature. It was a road of long usage dating from mid 1760's, when it began carrying much commercial trade between Pittsburgh and the Baltimore seaport. Scheduled stagecoach service began using this road in 1831. Zeigler, G. Fred, The Waynesburg, Greencastle and Mercersburg Turnpike; Kittochtinny Historical Papers, Volume XVII, Chambersburg, PA. 1981.

3   O.R. Series 1, Vol. 27 (Part II), pg 498ff; Tanner's Report.

4   The Monterey Springs Hotel had a long and checkered history as a store, stage stop, wagon tavern and hotel under various owners and managers dating from shortly after the revolution. The building at this time (1863) had been newly built after its predecessor was destroyed by fire in 1849 and was named The Monterey Springs Hotel in 1850 by the then owner, Samuel Buhrman. It was this resort hotel that became the temporary headquarters of both the Union and Confederate armies July 4-5, 1863. It was used as a hospital for some time after the retreat. Village Record, Waynesboro, PA, June 30, 1853, see also: Ibid-March 25, 1858 and The Record-Herald Waynesboro, PA, July 7, 1942.

Monterey Springs Hotel

This hotel changed possession as headquarters between the Union and Confederate armies at least four times during the Lee's Gettysburg campaign. It was newly rebuilt after a disastrous fire in 1849. It was also used as a hospital by both armies.

Union and Confederate] had spent the night bivouacked in the fields, woods and swamp surrounding the hotel. From about 1 a.m. the morning of July 5, 1863, after a muddy 19 hour march from the battlefield at Gettysburg, these soldiers had rested for three hours and resumed a march which lasted 14 hours to the south of Hagerstown by way of Waynesboro.[5] At the hotel, there were lines and queues of all sorts. Officers were waiting to dine; officers were waiting to bathe or to get a shave. There were also

---

5   Alexander, E.P., <u>Military Memoirs of the Confederacy</u>, Scribners, N.Y.C., NY, 1907, p. 436 ff.

droves of Union prisoners waiting to be paroled. The parole[6] was the main thrust of General Lee's coming there as was the content of the dispatch that he had received, while at Benchoof's, a short time before. The dispatch he had received was in reference to a reply to his battlefield request sent through the lines to General Meade,[7] under a flag of truce, while still at Gettysburg, that an exchange of prisoners be made. Meade's answer to this request

---

6   Faust, Patricia L. Editor, Encyclopedia of the Civil War, Harper and Row, NY, 1988.
    Parole was a means for dealing with large numbers of captured troops, early in the war, (A cartel agreed upon on September 22, 1862 and USA Gen. Orders #142, published September 25, 1862) by the U.S. and the Confederate governments (Gen. John A. Dix representing the USA and Gen. D.H. Hill representing the Confederacy) relied on the traditional European system of parole and exchange of prisoners. The terms of parole called for prisoners to give their word that they would not take up arms against their captors until they were formally exchanged for an enemy captive of equal rank. (Or, at least, it seemed so theoretically) "Enlisted men were to be exchanged man for man; officers were exchanged on the same basis, but according to rank on a complex scale of values: 2 lieutenants for 1 captain, 6 privates for 1 captain, 30 enlisted men for a general, and so forth. Surplus prisoners were to be paroled until they could officially be exchanged. Paroled soldiers were not to bear arms or perform military duties (that would release another soldier to active duty). Any differences (of opinion) that might arise out of the cartel would become the 'subject of friendly discussions' while the exchange continued".
    Robertson, James I., Soldiers Blue and Gray, U of S.C. 1988. Parole was supposed to take place within ten (10) days of capture. Generally, it was granted within a few days, especially after a major battle when thousands of prisoners were involved. Sometimes parolees went home to await notice of their exchange, sometimes they waited near their commands until the necessary paper work was processed.

7   Meade, George G., Major General-- Dispatch of July 4, 1863 at10 p.m. to Halleck: OR Series #1; Vol. 27; p. 78: "Major-General Halleck: No change of affairs since dispatch of 12 noon. I make a reconnaissance to-morrow, to ascertain what the intention of the enemy is. My cavalry are now moving toward the South Mountain Pass and should the enemy retreat, I shall pursue him on his flanks. [P.S]----A proposition made by General Lee, under a flag of truce, to exchange prisoners was declined by me."

was in the negative, pleading that he had no authority to agree to such terms and that an agreement must necessarily come from either General in Chief, H.W, Halleck or Secretary Stanton in the War Department in Washington.

General Lee's urgency to reach Monterey was to rescind his order to grant paroles to Union prisoners that he had given to Col. John W. Fairfax, who was at that moment taking oaths of parole at the hostelry. Lee had "borrowed" Fairfax of General Longstreet's staff and had sent him ahead strictly for this purpose, which would relieve the pressure on the retiring Confederate army of the responsibility of guarding, feeding and nursing between 4000 and 6000 Union prisoners. This would be a great burden to any army on the move.

General Longstreet's staff consisted of his Chief of Staff, G. Moxley Sorrel, a bank clerk of Savannah, Georgia, a Brigadier General by the age of twenty-six, but still a Colonel at the time of Gettysburg; Major J. W. Fairfax, (his volunteer Adj. General), Major P.T. Manning; and Captains Thomas Goree and Thomas Walton; and Lt. R. W. Blackwell.[8]

Of Longstreet's staff, "Undoubtedly the most vivid and refractory character among (them) was Colonel John W. Fairfax, scion of the old Virginia Fairfaxes, brave as any man in Lee's army, always in front of the firing and 'fond of his bottle, his Bible and his baths'. All through the campaigns he carried a tin hat, which served him as a wash basin. Neatly groomed and in every respect handsome, he was delighted to be mistaken for Longstreet, (who

---

8   Longstreet, James P., Gen.; SHSP, Vol. 3, p 279; Report.

was) one of the more handsome physical specimens of the service... Guarded more closely than anything except the honor of the Confederacy was Fairfax' chest, which held his liquor...Fairfax would open it for five or six nips when he took a bath before breakfast. An auxiliary supply of whiskey might invariably be found in the linen "housewife" or sack with two pockets, which hung conveniently in his tent. In one pocket he kept his bottle, in the other his Bible. Sunday was his "maudlin day" when (he) would lie around with his bottle and read his Bible."[9] Fairfax[10] was called off from taking the parole oaths and the prisoners already paroled were gathered up and placed in ranks under guard and herded onward toward Williamsport and the river.

An interesting first-hand account of the retrograde march of Union prisoners is given by Albert Wallber, 1st Lt. and Adj., of the 26th Wisconsin Infantry, USV who was taken prisoner on the first day of Gettysburg while retreating from General Ewell's Confederate forces west and north of the town. "Lee's army retreated in two columns, Infantry and Artillery; taking the

---

9   Tucker, Glenn; Lee and Longstreet at Gettysburg, p. 184 ff
10 Ward W.C., Private, CSA; Co. G, 4th Alabama, Law's Brigade, Confederate Veteran, Vol.8 p. 345 August, 1900. John Walter Fairfax was a Virginia gentleman whose home in Loudon County, had been the home of James Monroe, once President of the United States; (he was) a descendant of Thomas Lord Fairfax, who, in the (1700's) had removed from England and settled in the state of Maryland. Colonel Fairfax had been opposed to secession, was a man of great wealth, living in elegant splendor. Having made provision for his family during the time he expected the war to continue, he cast his fortunes with the South and took a position as a Volunteer Aide on the staff of General Longstreet and maintained himself while serving in the Army." He was a man of great bearing and bravery, impeccable dress, mounted with magnificent horses and was thoroughly reliable. He, through his bravery under fire, had become a favorite of General Lee.--

prisoners as a third column flanked by the infantry. As the roads for such a mass of men, guns and vehicles were not wide enough we were obliged to wander over rough fields, climb fences and wade through streams formed by the late rain. It was on July 5th that we reached Fairfield...Late the same day we came to the romantic South Mountains with their vales and ravines. Here want of room often pressed us together like hugh (sic) coils, which rolled on distressfully slow. The night was pitch dark and great caution had to be exercised not to be run over by horse and wagon... The morning of July 6th found us at Monterey Springs, a bathing place, where the rebels renewed negotiations for our parole. They saw how difficult it was to transport so many prisoners, that a strong escort would necessarily be required therfor (sic) which they would make use of better elsewhere and finally they seemed to fear an attack of our (Union) army resulting in our escape. They called us together and renewed the Gettysburg proposition. We consulted. Owing to General Halleck's order and noticing their anxiety to get rid of us, we promptly declined their offer.

"The failure of these negotiations brought us on the march again and a very tiresome one it was toward Waynesboro and Hagerstown on July 6th. It was a terrible night. Our column moved but slowly, halting about every five minutes.

"But, no rest was given us. Emaciated by scanty rations and hardly able to stand, we, dropped, on the muddy road, every time the procession halted, using every minute to steal a little sleep."[11]

---

11   Bandy and Freeland, Editors. The Gettysburg Papers, Vol. 1, pp. 358-359,
     Morningside Bookshop Press, 1978.

This question of the treatment of prisoners and parole became a political football for both of the opposing governments. Accusations of ill treatment of prisoners were flung back and forth by both sides during and for many years after the war.

On the third day of the Battle of Gettysburg, the War Department of the United States issued General Order No. 209 which stated in part, "Article 2 — It is understood that captured officers and men have been paroled and released in the field by other than commanders of the opposing armies and that the sick and wounded in the hospitals have been so paroled and released in order to avoid guarding and removing them, which in many cases would have been impossible. Such paroles are in violation of general orders and the stipulations of the cartel (of July 22, 1862) and are null and void. They are not regarded by the enemy and will not be respected by the Armies of the United States…"[12]

To which General J. A. Early commented after the War, "It is very manifest that that order was issued for the purpose of embarrassing General Lee's army with the guarding and feeding of the prisoners, amounting to several thousand, then in our hands; and in consequence of the order, information of which reached us immediately. General Lee sent a flag of truce to Meade on the 4th of July, after the close of the battle, with the proposition to exchange prisoners. The latter declined the proposition, alleging a want of authority to make the exchange or from his own views of policy; he positively declined to entertain the proposition. I am not certain which."[13]

---

12 Townsend, E.D., Assistant Adj. Gen., SHSP, Vol. 1, p. 308.
13 Ibid, ANV, SHSP, Vol. 1, p. 309.

General Early further said that the Union War Department on "issuing the order of July 3rd, 1863, violated the laws of civilized warfare and the statement contained therein that the Confederate Government ("the enemy") had pursued the same course was a mere pretext to give color to his own unwarranted act. But for that order all the prisoners captured at Gettysburg, amounting to fully six thousand would have been paroled; and, in fact, the proper staff officers were proceeding to parole them and had actually paroled and released a large number of them, when the news came of the order referred to. Why did Mr. Stanton object to the parolling (sic) of those prisoners…if it was not to embarrass the Confederate Government with the custody and support of them, regardless of any consideration for their health or their lives?"[14]

"In actual practice, however, many of the paroled soldiers considered that they were through with the war and wanted no further part of it. They were difficult to keep in parole camps. A Union officer at Annapolis estimated that three-fourths of the men under his charge were stern shirkers and that not 500 of the men either knew or cared to which units they belonged. 'If the men in my camp were a sample of our army, he stated, we would have nothing but a mob of stragglers and cowards.

"With this collapse of the cartel, after Gettysburg the number of prisoners increased dramatically as did the number of prisons. Both sides converted everything they could find into military prisons; jails, training camps, warehouses, school buildings, even

---

14 Ibid.

open fields. It was a situation that became particularly acute for the South. The largest influx of prisoners came to them when the Confederacy's transportation and supply systems were disintegrating."[15]

"In the North were numerous places for prisoners. They located at points as follows: Alleghany, Pa.; Alton, Ill.; Camp Butler, Ill.; Camp Chase Oh.; Camp Douglas Ill.; Camp Morton, Ind.; Elmira, N.Y.; Fort Columbus, N.Y.; Fort Lafayette, N.Y.; Fort Warren, Md.; Fort Wood, N.Y.; Fort Pickens, Fla.; Point Lookout, Md.; Rock Island, Ill.; Johnston's Island, Oh.; Louisville, Ky.; Memphis and Nashville, Tenn.

"In the South, prisons were located at Americus, Ga.; Camp Sumter, Andersonville, Ga.; Atlanta, Ga.; Augusta, Ga.; Blackshear, Ga.; Cahaba, Ala.; Camp Lawton, Millen, Ga.; Camp Oglethorpe, Macon, Ga.; Charleston, S.C.; Charlotte, N.C.; Salisbury, N.C.; Raleigh, N.C.; Danville, Va.; Richmond, Va.; Belle Isle, Castle Thunder, Crews; Libby, Pemberton's, Scott's, and Smith's Factory.

"The supposition is likewise that these places were selected for the convenience of the Confederate government for purposes of safety from raids for the release of prisoners and for proper care of the same.

"The prison at Andersonville called Camp Sumpter (sic) was the most noted of the Confederate prisons. In this prison, there were more Union prisoners and more suffering than in any other prison in the Confederate States. There Captain Henry Wirz was

---

15 Robertson, James I., Jr., <u>Soldiers Blue and Gray</u>, University of South Carolina Press. Columbia, 1988.

in command and to him has been charged the alleged cruelties and crimes at the prison.

"It is undoubtedly true that there was much suffering in this prison, but it is hardly true that Capt. Wirz was responsible for all of it, if for any.

"He was Swiss by birth, a physician by profession and he came to America long before the war and located in New Orleans, La. He entered the Confederate army and was severely wounded in a battle, so as to bar him from active field service. He was assigned and detailed for duty as commanding officer at Andersonville prison.

"After the war he was charged by the Federal authorities with various crimes at the prison. He was taken to Washington and there held to trial by a military court, which condemned him to be hung and he was executed on the 10th of November 1865.

"The military court which tried and condemned Confederate Captain Henry Wirz was presided over by General Lew Wallace, who subsequently became famous as the author of <u>Ben Hur</u> which has been published in numerous editions and read by thousands of our people…

"The circumstances of the Confederate government rendered it practically impossible to give the prisoners all of their necessities…

"The United States was in far better condition and with more favorable circumstances for the proper care of prisoners, yet they allowed our Confederates soldiers to suffer severely, many of them being put to death without cause or reason… Many of them died from starvation and freezing as occurred at Elmira, N.Y., Fort Delaware, Del., and at Sandusky (Johnston's Island) Ohio."[16]

Death was the situation in the extreme; "soldiers assigned to detention camps frequently suffered (not only) from shortages of food and clothing and poor sanitation and were victimized by a criminal element among them.

"It was finally admitted that the war was being prolonged by returning men to the ranks through parole and exchange---which by 1863 was the Confederate army's principal means of maintaining troop strength---Federal authorities after the (Battle of Gettysburg) severely restricted the program. The alternative (there was no other) confining captured enemy troops to prison camps became the policy for both belligerents."[17]

Lee, after countermanding the order he had given Colonel Fairfax, the order he had given in the hope of speeding the progress of the march from the battlefield by lightening the heavy escort required to control the great number of prisoners. It was much against his wish to give the command that the Union prisoners be conducted back to Confederate territory. They were a great hindrance to the march considering the bad weather, the terrible condition of the roads and the poor condition of the wagons, animals and men and in addition, he had little or nothing to feed them and could not spare the men to guard them.

---

16 Rodgers, R., Prisoners of War North and South, SHSP, Vol 34; pg. 72-73, 1906.

17 Faust, Patricia L., Editor; Historical Times Illustrated Encyclopedia of the Civil War, Harper & Row, NY, etc. See also Lee's order to Fairfax: Report of a Prisoner, Clipping Book Vol. VI, GNMP Coll., p. 18, n.p.n.d.

Lee's stay at the Monterey Springs was a brief one, after countermanding the order he had given Fairfax up to an hour or little longer. There was scarcely time to discuss the events of the night before, to receive some reconnaissance reports and to issue a dispatch or two and no time to discuss the battle of the previous days, although General Lee was said to discuss the hostilities freely while riding along the road.

Lee and his company pushed on toward the tollhouse intersection where the Baltimore Pike, the Chambersburg Road and the Maria Furnace Road converged. They were geographically in the center of the place where the hostilities of the previous night took place. In latter years (after the year 2000) these hostilities came to be known as "The Battle of Monterey Pass". It was a noteworthy fracas, being the only military engagement carried out in Pennsylvania with the exception of the Battle of Gettysburg.

When the withdrawal from the Gettysburg battlefield began the previous evening, General Lee had split the retiring Confederates into two separate trains one under the command of General John D. Imboden that staged partially at a park on the Chambersburg Pike and partially at a lay-by on the Gettysburg to Fairfield Pike. Imboden's train, wagons turned into ambulances, carried mostly the wounded soldiers that could not walk or fend for themselves. Some of the latter split from the main army at Fairfield and made rendezvous with the Chambersburg bound part of the wagon train at Cashtown by way of the Orrtanna Road. The main body of the army train slowly moved through the narrow mountain roads of the Monterey or South Mountain Gap. The line of march for this train was directed by Lee and contained some wounded, but, was comprised mostly of his entire fighting force or what was left of it, Infantry and Artillery, cannon, limbers and ammunition along with several hundred forage wagons loaded with food supplies, excepting contingents of Virginia cavalry and mounted infantry that guarded Imboden's wagons.[18] By this time, there was very little in the way of shoes or clothing supplies, with the exception of a great deal of plunder gathered from the rich Pennsylvania farms and factories, this supply train drove before it a herd of 4000 head of appropriated cattle and horses that increased the daily ration of the private soldier from 1/4 of a pound of bacon daily before the Pennsylvania invasion to 1-1/2 pounds of beef per man daily after the battle.[19] The Cavalry (under Stuart) had been instructed to head back to Virginia along the eastern side of the South and Catoctin mountains to reconnoiter the movements of Meade's army and to provide protection for the left flank of the retreating trains.

Lee's Fairfield Gap force had slow going from the beginning. They had lay the entire day of July 4th along Seminary Ridge, artillery at the ready, but low on ammunition; the Infantry dug and constructed earthworks in expectation of the coming assault by Meade's forces. Meade's assault was not forthcoming and the two opposing Armies spent the entire day watching each other. Both combatants were expecting the other to move against them. It was not to be! The attack never came on the part of either army.

---

18 GNMP Collection, Clipping Book Vol. VI, p. 18, n.p.n.d.
19 GNMP Collection, Clipping Book, Vol. VI, pp. 61-62, <u>The Gettysburg Times</u>, December 5, 1897.

General Lee, fell back on his original plan of an offensive campaign to which he had agreed long before he reached Gettysburg.[20] He had expended his manpower and ammunition supply in the three previous days battle, with no hope of replenishing either. General Lee chose to order an organized withdrawal to the South Mountain in the hope of drawing Meade's forces into an open engagement.[21]

The army began its retreat about 4 p.m. on the 4th of July in the midst of a tremendous downpour of rain that kept up torrentially all night. Lee had given the order of march at about 1 p.m. on July 4th which was the 3rd Corps (A.P. Hill's) to take the lead, followed by Longstreet's 1st Corps and Ewell's 2nd Corps to provide the rear guard, the respective commands to interchange positions on a daily basis. General Imboden was to take command of the long train of wounded and proceed to Williamsport by way of Greenwood and Greencastle bypassing Chambersburg. Ewell had Gen. John B. Gordon deploy his brigade as rear pickets to fend off any threats to the rear of Imboden's slow moving column. Meade did make several half-hearted threatening feints of attack to the Confederates, as they were disappearing into the mountains at Fairfield and a force under General Horatio Wright pressed the 26th Georgia Brigade, which was deployed to guard either side of the Fairfield Gap. Just at twilight on the 4th of July there was a

---

20 Ross, Fitzgerald, A Visit to the Cities and Camps of the Confederate States, p. 67, William Blackwood and Sons, Edinburgh, 1958.

21 Lee, R.E., Gen'l; The Wartime Papers of R.E. Lee, Dowdey & Manarin, Virginia Civil War Commission, Little, Brown & Co., Boston, 1st Edition, 1961, General Orders No. 74, p. 539.

lively skirmish at the rear of the Confederate column but the Yankees were easily driven back. Then Rodes Division of Ewell's Corps consisting of North Carolina and Georgia troops slammed the door shut on the gap for the night by bivouacking across the opening of the defile, at the foot of South Mountain.

Fairfield Gap

Lee's ANV retreat route, Jack's Mountain on left; Culp's Ridge on right; (center distance) Kepner's Knob. Upward of 25,000 soldiers, wagons, livestock and artillery passed through this narrow defile during the withdrawal. Lee had prudently prepared an offensive to seal off this route from a Union attack on his rear.

On the morning of the 5th, they awoke to find a line of union skirmishers, one and a half to two miles long spread across the valley floor to the north and south of Fairfield, that force of the 6th Army Corps of General Sedgewick, under Maj. General Horatio Wright had started from the vicinity of the Wheatfield perhaps as early as 4:30 a.m. that morning and soon advanced on the Confederates.[22] This attack was handily repulsed by General Daniel's North Carolinian's and General Dole's Georgians with little loss. The Union troops fired an half-hearted artillery barrage after the rear guard but had found the mouth of the pass so well fortified that they never ventured close enough to be in range of the rebel artillery. This contingent of Yankees marched on to Emmitsburg where Neill's Brigade was dispatched to pursue the withdrawing force in the Monterey Gap from the east along the Baltimore Pike. This "brigade" never showed itself to the Confederate rear guard and must have pursued from afar off.[23] Talk about having hell, the troops in advance of this rear guard had it in "spades" from the minute they hit the mountain roads leading through the South Mountain. The rain had been falling torrentially from the beginning of the retreat. Some of the descriptions of this retreat are real horror stories.

Colonel E. P. Alexander said, "Shortly after noon about 4 p.m. on the 4th before the head of the train was put in motion from Cashtown. Meanwhile, what would seem a visitation of the wrath of God had come upon us, had we not preferred the theory, which has been previously referred to, that storms may be generated by heavy firings. Now there came suddenly, out of the clear sky of the day before, one of the heaviest rainfalls I have ever seen. Probably four inches of water fell within 12 hours and it was sure to make the Potomac unfordable for a week."

---

22 Porter, John T., Editor, <u>Under the Maltese Cross Campaigns of the 155th Pennsylvania Regiment</u>, Pittsburgh, 1910, p. 203.
23 Purifoy, John, SHSP, Vol. 33; 1925, p. 338.

"Imboden, in <u>Battles and Leaders</u> gives the following description—'Shortly after noon on the 4th, the very windows of heaven seemed to have opened. The rain fell in blinding sheets, the meadows were soon overflowed and fences gave way before raging streams. During the storm, wagons, ambulances and artillery carriages by hundreds----nay, by the thousands---- were assembling in the fields along the road from Gettysburg to Cashtown in one confused and inextricable mass. As the afternoon wore on, there was no abatement of the storm. Canvas was no protection against the fury and the wounded men, lying upon the naked boards of the wagon-bodies were drenched, horses and mules were blinded and maddened by the wind and water and became almost unmanageable."[24]

"Imboden's train, Lee has since said, was nearly seventeen miles long. If it were possible for a man to have looked from a balloon at midnight on that army and its trains struggling through the merciless storm over those slippery mountain roads, a vision would have been revealed that no artists skill ever could place upon canvass (sic). Although the column was in motion the entire night, little progress was made; such was the impassable condition on the roads. Wagons broke down and horses and mules gave out and neither threats nor entreaties could urge them further. Half a dozen mules were at times hitched to single field gun to drag it out of the mud that clung like glue to everything that sunk into its depths. Wagons and improvised ambulances

---

24 Alexander, Edward P., Col., Military Memoirs of the Confederacy, Johnson, Robt. V., Edit., Scribners, N.Y. 1907, p. 436 quoting – Imboden, John D., Gen., Battles and Leaders of the Civil War, Century Co., N.Y. 1887-8.

broke down and were destroyed with axes where they stood or were hurled over embankments. The rear of Lee's army did not leave Gettysburg until the morning of the 5th and the march continued all that day."[25]

Lee's decision to return to Virginia was not an admission of defeat. He concluded that "Owing to the strength of the enemy's position and the reduction of our ammunition (Lee was still waiting to be re-supplied. He had depended heavily on a captured ammunition supply that he would have obtained in victory.) A renewal of the engagement could not be hazarded and the difficulty of procuring supplies rendered it impossible to continue longer where we were."[26] Lee gave Meade plenty of opportunity to pursue him and to give battle. In fact, it appears there is nothing Lee would have liked more. Meade felt that the mountain passes were too heavily fortified by the confederate's rear guard and preferred to shun Lee's trap. The rebel army was a seasoned bunch and were superb fighters and at their best when fighting the defensive battle. They had proven this many times in the past.

The design of General Lee in invading the Northern States was to free Virginia of the presence of the enemy--- to transfer the

---

25 GNMP Collection Clipping Book, Vol. VI, p. 18, n.p.n.d.

26 O.R. Series 2, Vol. 27, p. 309, See also Fremantle, A.J. L., Lt. Col., Coldstream Guards; Six Months in the Confederate States, Wm. Blackwood & Sons, Edinburgh & London, 1863. Before Gettysburg, Fremantle states, p. 246, June 27, 1863, "I was told this evening the numbers which have crossed the Potomac, also, the number of pieces of artillery. There is a large train of ammunition; for if the army (CSA) advances any deeper into the enemy's (USA) country, General Lee cannot keep his communications open to the rear and the staff officers say 'In every battle we fight, we must capture as much ammunition as we use'."

theatre of war to the enemy's country and to take the reasonable chance (and it was more of a gamble than a chance) of defeating his adversary there---knowing full well that to obtain an advantage there over the union would operate more powerfully in our (the Confederacy's) favor than to discomfit him in Virginia."[27]

As for the soldier's march itself and the conditions that attended it; there is no shortage of testimony. From a 6th North Carolina Regiment diary comes: "We were all day on the 5th making the short distance between Gettysburg and the foot of the mountains and we were not seriously molested by any pursuit until late in the evening, after sundown, when we were well in the mountains. The enemy ran up on a hill in our rear and threw a few shells at us, but, when we deployed and started towards him, he suddenly fell back and we were molested no more."[28]

John Simmons Shipp, a private soldier in Company "G", 6th Virginia Infantry gives us a graphic diary account of his service at Gettysburg to the crossing of the Potomac. He wrote in longhand:

> "July 3rd---Fighting commenced until sunrise and lasted till dark. It was more fierce than the day before. Both sides fought desperately. The enemy have a fine position on hills and their artillery fire is terrible. We the (*Army of the Confederacy*) have a little breast work, which was hit 23 times today and pieces of shell fell all

---

27 SHSP, Chapter 2; Vol. 4, p. 82; Taylor, Walter H.A.A.G.; <u>Causes of Lee's Defeat at Gettysburg</u>, 1877.

28 GNMP Collection, Vertical File 7, CS-9, Vol. 1, pp. 311-314; pp. 316-318, n.p.n.d.

around, nearly covering us with dirt. We have lost many men but at this time I don't know how many. We remained in the trench all day and all night. It is very hot.

"July 4th---Watching today nothing else doing. Both sides burying the dead. It is raining. F.H. and myself were fired at this morning by about a dozen skirmishers and the balls flew about our heads and cut the dirt up at our feet. At dark, we started to march and continued to march until 3 o'clock of the 5th p.m. It was horrible terrible dark, rainy, mud nearly knee deep. Roads full of rocks and pebbles, the worst I ever saw. At 12 o'clock at night we passed through the town of Fairfield, then we came to the mountains and got to the top about sunrise on the 5th. We saw where the enemies (sic) cavalry had captured the wagons of Ewell's Corps. We then went to guard a mountain pass, wet, tired and sleepy. Here is Monterey Springs in a valley among the mountains. 3 roads lead from the beautiful hotel to lovely scenery of hills, valleys and streams. I got a good supper here,

"At sunset, Longstreet's Corps came up and we started to march all night, or so we thought about 9 o'clock. F.H., I.K. and myself dropped out of ranks and stopped in a barn where at least 3 bushel of fleas feasted on us all night. I never felt or saw so many, but I slept very well. The first I had for 40 hours.

"6th---Started at daybreak and came up to the Regt.
at sunrise and camped at Frogtown[29] Rocks till 5 p.m.
when we started and marched through the towns of

---

29 Frogtown was an early colloquial name for Pikesville, a string of houses along the
    Mercersburg, Greencastle and Waynesboro Turnpike, a toll road established by an
    Act of Legislature in 1808 in Franklin County, Pennsylvania. This village of
    Frogtown/Pikesville became Rouzerville, a US Post Office established in 1873, a
    decade after the Battle of Gettysburg and is still so named today and is now the
    center of extensive commercial and residential development. There are two
    theories advanced by early residents as to why it was called Frogtown. The first
    being that adjacent to this settlement there was an extensive marsh. It is a
    floodplain of Red Run, which is a tributary of the East Branch of the Little
    Antietam Creek. This marsh was thickly populated by frogs, toads, spring
    peepers, chorus and cricket frogs. Some of these species live through the winter
    freeze. They subsist on sucrose stored in their bodies and "peep" all winter. In
    early spring and summer this frog chorus sometimes reached a deafening pitch.
    This marsh is now drained through public works and by a lowering water table.
    We can remember ice-skating many times on the flooded land. The second theory
    is Peter Rouzer of French descent was a truck farmer, huckster, storekeeper,
    sawmiller/lumber dealer, tanner and sometime speculator and the main builder
    and developer of the homes along the Turnpike. Thus he became the namesake
    for the Post Office. This second theory holds that since Rouzer was of French
    descent and the derogatory term for a Frenchman was "frog", since the French
    consider frog legs a delicacy. A further explanation behind the epithet is that in
    early France the peasants lived on the low, marshy ground; while the nobles lived
    on the higher ground and called the peasants "le grenouille" hence "a frogtown".
    We would favor the first theory as advanced, since it pre-dates both Pikesville and
    Rouzerville and The War of the Rebellion.
    Frogtown Rocks are those group of rocks along present day Old Pennsylvania
    Route 16, (the WGM Turnpike) that lie along the rocky, precipitous sides of the
    highway just above Rouzerville and that group of rocks lately (turn of the 20th
    century) known as Lovers Rocks, which are now, and were then, on private
    property and in olden days were a popular sparking and picnic ground. We have
    one other reference to Frogtown—"There was nothing done on the 4th of July.
    Late in the evening, I received orders to draw off the division as soon as it became
    dark and take the road toward Fairfield. On the fifth I was directed to hold the
    gap in the mountains between Fairfield and Waynesborough. In the evening, (5th)
    I moved to a place called Frogtown, at the (western) base of the mountain."
    Zeigler, G. Fred, The Waynesburg, Greencastle and Mercersburg Turnpike;
    Kittochtinny Historical Papers, Volume XVII, Chambersburg, PA. 1981. Local
    tradition.

42

Waynesborough and two other villages the names of which I did not learn. The people are all Union. The ladies wear Union badges around their necks and look very grim at us. Slept in a woods, in an old barn about 12 o'clock this night. We passed a distillery and a few found it out and filled canteens with it. I started to get some but the Provost Guard had seized it. 66 bbls. I got a taste of it, strong ast (sic) aqua fortis.[30]

Courtesy of Mary Ann McCleaf Potter

Pikesville Ca 1910

Snapshot of Pikesville Hill taken about 1910, this scene was very little changed until the 2000 millennium, the first decade of which saw many new developments. This hill and pike would have been viewed by Lee and his army as they turned toward Waynesborough.

---

30 Aqua Fortis (strong water) being nitric acid ($HNO3$) a very strong fuming acid; when combined with Hydrochloric acid (HCl), it forms aqua regia (royal water); it is the only combination of acids that will dissolve gold

"7th---We are now 1 mile from Hagerstown cooking three days rations. Stayed here all day the cavalry are scouting and skirmishing all around in a beautiful country. The whole artillery is here."[31]

Photo courtesy of Hazel Adams Schaeffer

Monterey Tollhouse Ca 1892

Monterey or Mount Zero Tollhouse as it looked in 1892. The parasol lady (rt) is Harriett Benchoff Brown, a nigh dweller, she was Billie Benchoff, the Provost Marshal's daughter. Some of the heaviest fighting took place at this site. It was also used as a hospital. The Confederates turned the turnpikers out of their home to treat the wounded. There were several Rebel burials on the near side of the road, which were later disinterred.

31 Shipp, John Simmons, Pvt., ANV, Co "G", 6th Virginia Infantry, Holographic Diary 4 in. x. 3 in., Virginia Historical Society (Battle Abbey) Library, Mss2, SH646 – Diary from May 10, 1862 to March 31, 1864.

As Lee, Longstreet and company rode along the Monterey Road they approached the tollhouse intersection of three roads that John Shipp described in his diary, It was at this intersection that Kilpatrick's Cavalry first struck the center of the Confederate wagon train in retreat and decimated it from this point to Ridgeville (now Ringgold, MD) which was about 9 miles away.

Lee and his officers knew all about this taking of prisoners and burning of wagons but we doubt if he ever considered to call it the Battle of Monterey after the three-day strife that his army had just experienced. The tollhouse itself was one owned by the WGM Turnpike Company and its turnstile stood at the intersection of the Old Furnace Road from Fairfield and Gettysburg; the Mentzer Gap or Chambersburg Road and the Emmitsburg to Waynesboro Turnpike. This was the beginning place of the disruptive attack that had begun a mile or two east of the Monterey Springs Hotel on this self-same highway, that stormy night before this day's sun began to shine.

CHAPTER THREE

The Toll Was Paid In Lives

As Lee, Longstreet and staff sloshed and sloughed westward from the Monterey House toward the tollhouse the debris of the engagement at Monterey became more and more evident. As they approached the gatehouse, the road could not have been in poorer condition, it became rougher, muddier and cut by the troughs left by the horses and thousands of livestock, cannon and limber, wagons and marching men that had traveled over it during the previous night. In the nearby forest, could be heard the bellows of stray cattle, the brays of mules, and the bleating of lost sheep that been frightened off by the fierce storm and the attack of the Union cavalry the night before and which were now adrift in the forest searching for food and the safety of the number of the herds of which they had been a part.

Lee said, "It is a sad affair." glancing aside at the wounded men struggling to walk along the rough road. He mused, "We are losing our army to stragglers and those people in Washington are using the parole cartel as a weapon to encumber us with Union (prisoners) mouths to feed. I can always rely on my Army for fighting, but its discipline is poor." At the time of the Maryland invasion Lee had lost more than twenty-five thousand men from straggling alone and he exclaimed with tears, 'My army is ruined by straggling.' [1]

As they approached the gate intersection the rubble and wreckage of previous night's engagement became evident. There was a wrecked cannon dominating the center of the roadway. There was battle debris, broken wagons and dead or wounded horses along the way. The tollgate house, now a hospital, was surrounded by wounded men and there were several dead

---

[1] Alexander, Edward Porter, *Southern Historical Society Papers*, Volume 9, 1881, p 514.

Lee after the rebuff of his field proposal to Meade for the exchange of prisoners became much exorcised over the losses that his Army was sustaining from the lack of discipline, straggling and desertion. Statistics and "revelations of the actual condition of the Army of Northern Virginia since the close of the war do not justify this assertion" (That the Confederates were ascribed a degree of discipline, even higher than that of the Army of the Potomac) "On the contrary, they show that the discipline of (the Southern Army) was never equal to that of the Army of the Potomac, though in fire and *élan* (eagerness) it was superior."

An inspection of the records of Confederate regiments after the Battle of Gettysburg bears out Alexander's assertion. After Gettysburg, individual soldier's cachets abound with notations such as "no further [military] record"; "deserted to the enemy"; "took oath of allegiance", "not present or accounted for after (date)." It is obvious that after this battle many soldiers of the south had had enough of the war. Such was the impact of this enormous conflict. This battle had broken the back of the Confederate army and, in addition, had taken an enormous toll on the Union army.

Confederate soldiers lying in the field across the road opposite the house. [2]

Local legend has it that where the rhododendron bushes grow opposite the old tollhouse was the burial site of two Confederate soldiers. The tollhouse is probably the oldest house now standing at Blue Ridge Summit, with perhaps the exception of founder Patrick Mooney's stone house on the present day Jacob's Church Road, possibly the log cabin next to the tollhouse, (John Wesley Brown house) just north of it. The bloodstains of the wounded

---

2   Raiford, Neil Hunter, The 4th North Carolina in the Civil War, McFarland and Co.; Jefferson, NC; 2003.
The Tollgate house was used as a hospital after the Monterey skirmish and two 4th North Carolina Cavalrymen died there and were buried on the east side of the turnpike opposite the building, they were Corporal Wm. H. Flowers, Co. "C", 4th North Carolina who died in the house on July 5, 1863. He was 28 years old and from Wilson, NC, He was an illiterate farm laborer and Pvt. John Dempster, Co "E" 4th N.C. Cavalry, 43 years old, probably a Virginian. Dempster had been killed in action during the skirmish at Monterey, the night of July 4, 1863, when Kilpatrick's Cavalry had charged the wagon train. These men were disinterred from the tollhouse site in May, 1866 and removed to Gettysburg under the direction of the Dr. John W.C. O'Neal, who was in charge of re-burials. Their remains were directed to be returned to the South and both remain buried in the Confederate Section of historic Oakwood Cemetery in Raleigh, N.C. There were several men wounded in the Monterey skirmish from Companies "C' and "E" of the 4th North Carolina Cavalry: one of them was Sgt. Patrick H. Hand of Co. "C", he was a 35 year old farmer, of New Hanover County, NC. He recovered and fought through the Valley Campaigns and was at the surrender at Appomattox, where he was paroled on April 9, 1865.
The re-interments of Confederate dead continued, under the direction of the U.S. government, for a decade or more after the close of the battle: Village Record (Waynesboro, PA) Issue of July 17, 1873: "The remains of about 350 Confederate soldiers from the battlefield of Gettysburg were recently taken to Baltimore over the Northern Central Railway. Nearly all the dead were destined for Richmond. These remains (with the exception of a few to be brought on next fall) comprise the remnant of the Confederate dead at Gettysburg, The entire number buried there having been about 3400."

soldiers remained on the floors of the gatehouse until well into the 20th century. The wooden pump that stood in the yard of the tollgate house is now preserved as an artifact at the Renfrew Museum in Waynesboro.

This turnpike house had (by proxy) figured in another incident early in the spring of that year. According to the newspaper <u>Village Record</u> (Waynesboro, PA), March 6, 1863, a Union deserter was shot near Buena Vista.

Summary: Last Saturday, Samuel Wade of Co. "A", 77th Regiment PA Volunteers was shot near Buena Vista Springs while trying to escape from the Provost Guard who had arrested him earlier. Though serious, the piece relates, Wade's wounds are not life threatening.

Samuel Wade, was a turnpiker and kept the tollgate at Monterey and maintained the road surface. He was 48 years old and it is supposed that when he was away serving in the militia, his wife Mary and his mother-in-law, Elizabeth Lamb, collected the tolls.[3]

The carnage had begun directly after the Lee's Army had begun to withdraw from the Gettysburg Battle and the Union 3rd Cavalry Division under the command of General Hugh Judson Kilpatrick, comprised of two brigades, was ordered by General Pleasonton at 10 a.m. on July 4th, 1863 to move in pursuit of the Confederates by their left flank, along the South Mountain (Jack's), by way of

---

3   U.S. Federal Census on Microfilm for 1860 – Franklin County, Washington Township, PA, p. 41.

the road from Gettysburg to Emmitsburg and then through Fountaindale toward the Monterey Pass, where they were ordered to intercept the retreating army train and destroy it, if possible. It was by this order that Kilpatrick had learned that Lee's army was in full retreat.

Kilpatrick's First Brigade had been lately commanded by Brigadier General Elon Farnsworth, one of his so called "Boy Generals" who was killed on the 3rd of July at Gettysburg while gallantly leading a charge that attempted to thwart the Confederate reinforcement of Pickett's charge. Farnsworth's cavalry attempt was, more or less, a suicidal attack made through withering enemy crossfire, under direct orders from Kilpatrick to a reticent Farnsworth, who was well aware that he and his cavalry were doomed in facing such devastating battle odds. The charge did ultimately play a key role in the stopping the Pickett's reinforcement.

With Farnsworth dead, his 1st Brigade was now under the command of Col. Nathaniel P. Richmond of the 1st West Virginia Cavalry USA and the Brigade comprised the 1st West Virginia, the 18th Pennsylvania Cavalry, the 1st Vermont Cavalry and the 5th New York Cavalry. Major Charles Capehart took Farnsworth's regimental command with Captains Farabee and Carman acting as his Majors.

The 2nd Brigade was under the command of General George Armstrong Custer, another of Kilpatrick's newly commissioned "Boy Generals" and was made up of troopers of the 1st, 2nd, 5th, 6th and 7th Michigan Cavalries.

General Custer was the most dashing cavalryman ever to serve in the United States Army. He was 23 years old at the time of the Battle of Gettysburg and had graduated from the United States Military Academy at West Point, by the skin of his teeth. His class standing had been one notch below last in his class.[4] It is a fact that his name had been withdrawn from the roster of June, 1861 graduates and re-instated at the last minute, no reason given, probably because the administration couldn't conceive of putting up with him for another year. He was a singular character, nonetheless, an innovative and fearless warrior and intrepid leader of men. He stood 5 feet 8 1/2 inches tall and weighed 170 pounds. He had light blue eyes and sandy blond hair. He had been born raised a farm boy in New Rumley, Ohio,

Frederick Whittaker - Custer - 1876

Custer

George Armstrong Custer, Brigadier Gen. whose 2nd Michigan Volunteer Cavalry spearheaded the destruction of the retreating Confederate Army and wagon train from Monterey Springs to Ringgold a distance of more than nine miles. The Union could have shortened the conflict with a few more soldiers with Generals like Custer.

---

4   <u>Evening Herald</u>, Hanover, PA; Friday, June 30th 1899, GNMP Clipping Book, Vol. VI, p. 75.

on December 5, 1839. At the time of the Battle of Gettysburg and he had been brevetted Brigadier General on 29 June 1863, less than a week before the Battle. He was unmarried at that time.

"Fighting for fun is rare." said Col. Theodore Lyman, member of General George G. Meade's staff, only such men as Custer and a few others, attacked whenever they got a chance and of their own accord..."[5]

"Custer was a dandy in reverse almost what the Sioux called a "contrary". With his slouched Confederate hat, he made it a practice of cutting his hair and then letting it grow long [shoulder-length] and smearing it with cinnamon oil, his hodge-podge uniform [was] forever in need of washing and his [he wore] over-sized boots."[6]

---

5   Agassiz, George R., Editor, Meade's Headquarters, 1863-1865, Atlantic Monthly Press, Boston, 1922, p. 139. See also Barnett, Louise, K., Touched by Fire, Henry Holt, New York, p. 30, 1996,

6   Ambrose, Stephen E., Crazy Horse and Custer, Doubleday, New York, 1976, pp 161ff & 184ff.
    See also: Gregg, Rod, Old West Quiz and Fact Book, Perennial, Harper, Row & Co., New York, 1986.
    "He took to wearing captured Confederate boots, the bigger, the better. This outlandish footwear provided a standing joke (for his comrades). He carried a 50 caliber Springfield carbine and two British Webley "Royal Irish" side arms. His "uniform" was a light velveteen "hussar" jacket with five gold loops on each sleeve and a sailor shirt with a very large collar...the shirt was a dark blue and with it he wore a conspicuous red tie. He wore tight black trousers trimmed with gold lace, a soft Confederate slouch hat, that he had picked up on the field. His hair was long and in curls almost to his shoulders. A staff officer remarked that he looked like "a circus rider gone mad".
    "The bright red tie turned out to be the best touch of all; his staff, the, his field officers and finally the enlisted men all took to wearing a red neckerchief and it became a distinguishing mark of the men of the 2nd Michigan Calvary Brigade. A Captain once thought that Custer must have been a courier or an aide, not a commanding general. Circus rider gone mad, courier or not; George A. Custer was still

The day after the Battle of Gettysburg at 10 a.m. on July 4, 1863, Kilpatrick's troops moved toward Emmitsburg in Maryland with Custer's 2nd Brigade in the lead and Nathaniel Richmond's 1st bringing up the rear following the left flank of Lee's retreating army. They moved along the road from Gettysburg to Emmitsburg, where they engaged in a lively skirmish with the rear guard of Stuart's cavalry, that went quickly on the way toward Mechanicstown (Thurmont) not caring to put Kilpatrick's larger Union force to the test.

This was not the first time these antagonists had faced each other. The first time was at Aldie Station, Loudon County, VA on June 17, 1863 when the Michigan troops were in pursuit of Stuart's cavalry, that had been deployed to screen Lee's advance northward along the Shenandoah Valley toward the invasion of Pennsylvania. They caught up with Stuart at Hanover, PA on June 30, 1863, where Kilpatrick was forced back by the Confederates, but, ultimately the Union troops prevailed and drove Stuart from

---

Footnote #6 (Cont'd)

the most daring cavalryman that ever served in the U.S. Army. His worth to the Union may be judged when it is stated, that his command, in the last six months of the Civil War captured in battle, 65 battle flags, 7 general officers, 10,000 prisoners and 111 cannon without losing a gun or a flag"(See Footnote 8, *Evening Herald*, Hanover, PA p. 75) It was Custer's Cavalry Brigade that brought Lee's last stand to an abrupt halt at Appomattox Courthouse.

This was the same George A. Custer that had perished with all 274 of his men at the Battle of the Little Big Horn, near Billings, Montana on Sunday, June 25, 1876. The final details of his demise are of interest in themselves. His body was buried where it fell at the Battle of the Big Horn. A little over a year later, on July 2, 1877, it was disinterred, on command of Gen. John M. Schofield and sent up the Missouri River on the steamboat "Fletcher" to Fort Abraham Lincoln, North Dakota and then by rail to Poughkeepsie, N.Y. where it was buried at West Point Military Academy on October 19, 1877, the Rev. Dr. John Forsyth presiding.

the Hanover and York area. The two last met at Hunterstown, PA on July 2, 1863 and this was probably Custer's finest hour as a commandant and strategist.[7] General D. M. Gregg said that at Hunterstown, "Brigadier-General Custer commanding First [Second] Brigade, Third Division very ably assisted me in the duties of my command…"[8]

At Hanover, General Kilpatrick had sent a dispatch to General Pleasonton saying, "We have plenty of forage, the men are in good spirits and we do not fear Stuart's whole cavalry. P.S. General Lee is at Hagerstown."[9] On July 2nd, they routed Stuart's troopers on Cavalry Field as Stuart was on his tardy way to reinforce Lee who had been the while anxiously waiting for Stuart's reconnaissance. By this time, Lee was deeply engaged in conflict with Meade.

On June 26, 1863, when Meade was made the Commanding General of the Army of the Potomac replacing Hooker; Kilpatrick, only a few years older than Custer, was appointed as Division Commander under Pleasonton and had the stars to show for it. Custer was jealous of his old classmate, who was 27 years old and had graduated West Point in 1861, just six months before Custer. Custer set out to show that he was a better soldier than his old school rival and present commander. At the time of the Monterey engagement, he had been brevetted, by Kilpatrick, just a week before as a Brigadier General of Volunteers, along with Wesley Merritt and Elon Farnsworth, all young general officers (Merritt

---

7 O.R. Series 1, Vol. 27 (Part I), p. 957, Report of Brig. Gen. D. McM. Gregg. See also O.R., same series, p. 1000 Report of Brig. Gen. G. M. Custer.

8 O. R. Series 1, Vol. 27, (Part I), p. 987.

9 Ibid, O.R. Series 1, etc.

was 29 years old and had graduated from West Point in 1860. Farnsworth was 26 years old and not a West Pointer. His uncle, John F. Farnsworth was a powerful politician and an active civil war general). The leap of these three lower ranked [youngsters] from cavalry officers to generals has never been adequately explained.[10] They were probably given field commissions as part of Meade's attempt to revitalize the Union cavalry by replacing an older command with new and more daring blood.

After the Battle of Gettysburg, at 10 a.m., on July 4, 1863, Kilpatrick acting on orders from General Pleasonton moved with Custer's 2nd Brigade in advance and Richmond's 1st Brigade bringing up the rear, to the left of Lee's retreat, along the road from Gettysburg to Emmitsburg and then through Fountaindale toward the Monterey Pass, where they had been ordered to intercept the Confederate Army train and destroy it, if possible. This was Lee's vulnerable point in crossing the South Mountain. It was by this order Kilpatrick had first learned that the Confederates were in full retreat toward Virginia.

There was a brief skirmish at Emmitsburg with the rear guard of Stuart's cavalry but the Confederate guard went quickly on their way toward Mechanicstown [Thurmont] spurning to do battle with a superior force, while Custer's brigade made a sharp right at that place and turned toward the Monterey Gap and Springs. When they reached the tollhouse (still standing) at the inter-section of the Hagerstown-Gettysburg Turnpike with the

---

10 Evening Herald, Hanover, PA, Friday, June 30, 1899, GNMP Vertical File, Vol. VI, p. 75.

Waynesboro, Greencastle & Mercersburg Turnpike [Baltimore Pike] just east of Fountaindale, the 1st and the 5th Michigan Cavalry were sent to reconnoiter on this pike [present Jack's Mountain Road] at first, found nothing north of the intersection and then came upon line of pickets blockading the road, protecting the flank of Ewell's retreating train from Millerstown [Fairfield]. The rear guard was B.H. Robertson's 4th and 5th Virginia Divisions of J.E.B. Stuart's Brigade, that had been ordered to guard the train at all costs and to attempt to strike a blow on the Union cavalry if it threatened the retreating troops.

The charge was made on the Jack's Mountain Road blockade by a squadron of Custer's cavalry under Lt. Col. Peter Stagg of the 1st Michigan and a deadly action ensued. The enemy pickets were driven back and the Union held this by-road until the entire Union column had passed unharmed up the mountain. This took place shortly before dark on July 4th, 1863. Lt. Col. Stagg had his horse killed and sustained serious injuries in his fall from the horse. Capt. William Elliott was mortally wounded and Lt. James S. McIlhenny was killed. Private soldiers numbering 17 were also lost in this engagement.[11] This skirmish and Starr's return previous to it, was as deadly, if not more so than the action at Monterey. The Confederate pickets did not know that they had left the turnpike leading to Monterey wide open for Kilpatrick and his troops, save one impediment that awaited them at the top of the pass.

---

11 O.R. Series 1, Vol. 27, (Part I), p. 998, Custer.

To illustrate the variance of importance and viewpoint of soldiers and officers in the post-battle aftermath I would include here an undated account written by Major Luther S. Trowbridge of the 5th Michigan Cavalry written to the regimental historian sometime after the war, recounting the same encounter on the Hagerstown-Gettysburg Turnpike (Jack's Mountain Road).

"Capt. J. Allen Bigelow, Historian 5th Michigan Cavalry, Birmingham, Mich. My dear Capt.—I promised you sometime ago that I would write you something of the whereabouts of the 5th Michigan immediately succeeding the Battle of Gettysburg. You know so much about that Battle as I do, so I will let that pass.

"The next day – the 4th of July, I remember very distinctly being summoned with the other officers of the Division to Gen'l. Kilpatrick's headquarters and listening to a very inspiring little speech from that officer, who told us that we were to move at once to get around the flank of Lee's army and reach his trains, as he (Lee) was retreating to Virginia. I remember well the shout that was given by the men of the regiment when I reported what Genl. Kilpatrick had said.

"We took the Emmitsburg road – I suppose this was about 10 or eleven o'clock in the morning – and about noon it began to rain and how it did rain! I had been out in a good many rainstorms, but never before I think had seen it rain harder. It did not require a great

58

amount of sense or military skill to see that Fate or Providence was putting into the hands of the army (sic) of the Potomac, a great opportunity. The ditches along the road and the little streams that we crossed were filled to overflowing and it was evident enough that before night the Potomac would be bank full with no possibility of fording for some days to come. At Emmitsburg, Col. Alger, with his usual kindness and forethoughtfulness hurried to the post office to send letters to his wife and my wife to relieve them from the strain of anxiety which must have been very great.

"At Emmitsburg we turned to the west and when we reached the foot of Monterey Gap, I was sent with my battalion out on a road coming down from the north at the foot of the mountain (Jack's Mountain Road) to guard the flank of the column from any attack from that quarter. We moved about a mile, meeting with no serious opposition, but skirmishing with some wandering parties of the enemy or perhaps parties on outpost duty. We had not been there very long when an orderly came and said, "General Kilpatrick presents his compliments and directs that you hold this road at all hazards." I returned my compliments to the General and asked the orderly to say to him that so far there had been no appearance of any considerable party of the enemy and I had no doubt of my ability to hold the road. The orderly departed and about fifteen minutes afterward another came with the same message and received the same reply. He departed and soon after, a Captain of Artillery from the General's staff with the same message. I listened to him and then said, "All right, Captain, this is the third time I received that message within the last hour. I have seen nothing to lead me to think there is any considerable force of the enemy in my front and have so reported. If you have any information to the contrary, I would be glad to receive it."

"Oh, bless you," he replied, "Haven't you been told? Jones's Brigade is up this road somewhere and the General doesn't want him to come down on the flank of his column." On receiving this information, I made arrangements to give a warm reception to any force that might attempt to come that way. I moved Company "F" up the road about a quarter of a mile where I found a good place to find them behind a stone wall, where they had fine range down the road. I threw a barricade "across the road to check a charge and quietly awaited the approach of the enemy. We remained there until about ten o'clock (p.m.) when Lieut. Whittaker of Kilpatrick's staff came with an order for us to rejoin the command. The Division had long passed the road which I was to hold at all hazards and I noticed that Whittaker was quite nervous for fear we might come on some of the enemy's cavalry that might be following up

Kilpatrick. That fear was, however, groundless and about midnight we reached the top of the mountain at Monterey Pass."[12]

Lt. Colonel Stagg's cavalry squadron previous to Trowbridge's assignment, under orders from Custer, had lead a charge against Robertson's superior force and had driven them back to the Millerstown (Fairfield) Road and held them there before the Trowbridge's arrival. They were fortunate enough to miss the action. [13]

General Lee "had ordered Robertson and Jones to Fairfield, eight miles to the southwest, to counter a body of Yankee cavalry that had been seen heading toward a forage train in the army's rear. Lee wanted those wagons protected – he needed every ounce of rations, every pound of forage his men had gathered from the breadbasket known as southern Pennsylvania. When within a few miles of his destination Jones spied a small group of Yankee horsemen approaching from the southeast. Although it was difficult to determine numerical strength at such a distance, Jones could see that he outnumbered the newcomers. They proved to be about four hundred members of the 6th U.S. Cavalry, Maj. Samuel Starr commanding... A few miles south of town, (Emmitsburg) the brigade leader, Brig. Gen. Wesley Merritt, had detached them to capture the wagon train, whose location a civilian informant had reported that morning. The fight that

---

12 Trowbridge, Luther, Maj. 5th Michigan Cavalry, GNMP File 4-14, Undated letter to J. Allen Bigelow, Historian 5th Michigan Cavalry.

13 O.R. Series 1, (Part I), p. 957, Custer.

broke out in the shadow of South Mountain (along the Jacks Mountain Road) began when Jones charged the Union regulars with his lead regiment, the 7th Virginia. Lt. Col. Marshall's troopers butted into Starr's advance squadron and began to force it back, but at a critical moment another element of the 6th slammed into their flanks and thrust them back in turn.

Simultaneously, Maj. Starr dismounted his main body behind roadside trees and fences inaccessible to mounted men. From those positions, his men raked both [Confederate] flanks with carbine fire. Reeling from the volley, the Virginians milled about in the road, horses edging toward panic. Several mounts bolted to the lead; others caught the frenzy and soon the entire 7th Virginia was whirling to the rear, running a gauntlet of fire. One historian has speculated that by withdrawing they (the Confederates) absorbed more casualties 'than would have been lost had their onset been made with vigor and boldness.'

"By this time Maj. Starr had come to appreciate how badly he was outnumbered and out-positioned. He tried to remount his regiment and regain the road either to flee or launch a forlorn-hope counterattack. Before he could do either Flournoy's Virginians swarmed over his position and a slash-and-shoot contest erupted in the road and on both sides of it. Starr was wounded – he would lose an arm to amputation – and his little band was decimated. A few of the (Union) Regulars broke free from the writhing tangle and headed for the hills or for Fairfield in full retreat. Most, however, were shot down before they could reach safety. In the end, almost 250 Federals became casualties, most of them prisoners of war. The captives included Starr, two of his captains, four of his lieutenants and two of his surgeons.

"While the last fugitives were run to earth, Grumble Jones saw to it that the wounded portion of his 55 casualties received medical care, as did all injured prisoners. He also ensured that Starr and his luckless troopers were well guarded and questioned. Finally, he secured the wagon train he had been sent to protect and placed his brigade in bivouac not far from Jack's Mountain whose passes he and Robertson were tasked to guard.

"These passes – the shortest route from Gettysburg to Hagerstown and Williamsport, Maryland – had become extremely important to both armies…

"Then nature and the enemy combined to complicate matters. Rain that began late in the afternoon of Independence Day and refused to stop caused the Potomac to overflow its banks. Thereby preventing a fording operation at Williamsport. That same day a Union demolition party from Harper's Ferry (under Gen. French) raided the bridgehead at Falling Waters, chased off a guard detail from Massie's regiment and rendered the pontoon span unusable."[14]

To continue Trowbridge's narrative:

"You will perhaps remember that there was a large space of cleared land about a large hotel there. That space was filled with men and horses mixed in a great deal of confusion. The first person whom I saw to recognize was Colonel Alger who said to

---

14 Longacre, Edward A., <u>Lee's Cavalrymen, A History of the Mounted Forces of the Army of Northern Virginia (1861-1865)</u>, Stackpole, Mechanicsburg, PA, 2002, p.224ff.

me. 'I wish you would tell where my regiment is?' I replied, "Here is one battalion of it just arrived in good order." He went on and I turned my battalion out of the road – formed in close order – dismounted and waited for orders. I had been riding a mare of Major Ferry's and when I dismounted I discovered that she was pretty well used up. She dropped her head as if she could go no farther. My own horse had cast a shoe and was very lame. An order was received to move out at once and I did not know what to do for a horse. Just then a Sergeant of Co. "A" came up leading three or four captured horses and asked me what he should do with them. "Well," I said, "Give me the best one and turn the others over to your Quartermaster." He said, 'Here is one which I think from his trappings must be an officer's horse." He brought him up and I mounted the most comfortable saddle horse I had ever ridden. He was an ill-looking beast, but, a remarkable one to go."

"We moved out and I was passing by a gate, General Custer, who was standing there. Called out, 'What troops are these?' "The first battalion of the 5th Michigan Cavalry," I replied. 'All right, Major, I want you to get to the head of this column, (there was a long column of mounted men standing in the road) take command of the whole business and go ahead at a trot.' I did as I was ordered and as I hurried past the column, I cautioned each Company to keep well closed up, as we were going ahead at a trot. When I reached the head of the column, I gave the order to trot, when I heard away back toward the rear, 'Halt! Halt!' "No", I said, "We are ordered to go ahead at a trot" and away we went. The road was very slippery after the rains and being down hill, the horses slipped badly. I thought there must be a fight ahead, but I was soon undeceived. From the burning wagons on the side of the road, I knew that someone must have gone ahead of us. We marched until 4 o'clock a.m. destroying a large train and capturing many prisoners. We halted at Smithsburg to rest and feed.

"At Smithsburg, General Kilpatrick attempted to get his prisoners, of whom we had about 1900, back across the South Mountain in order to turn them over to the Infantry, but found the road occupied by the enemy (Stuart)."[15]

What Trowbridge did not know was that his was the clean-up brigade for the Battle of Monterey Pass. Having been to the rear in the action with Robertson's cavalry at Jack's Mountain and missed the heated skirmish with Emack at Monterey Heights.[16]

---

15 Trowbridge, Luther, Maj. USA 5th Michigan Cavalry, GNMP File 4-14, Undated letter to J. Allen Bigelow, Historian of the 5th Michigan Cavalry

16 <u>Clarification</u> is necessary to be given in regard to Monterey. There were two (2) Monterey Springs given in both narrative and in the Official Records (O.R.). There was the Monterey Springs Hotel, which was a large summer hotel near the summit of the Monterey Pass. This building served as headquarters for both Confederate, though not for General Lee, and was held for short time by them and by the Union forces and was for a short time, General Kilpatrick's headquarters. About a mile west of this Monterey Springs Hotel were the Monterey Springs (these springs have been known by various names over time, Rockey Springs, Brown's Spring, Rolando, etc.) The springs and bath houses were connected with the hotel, and mentioned often in Confederate and Union reports because they were located at the intersection of the roads, near the tollhouse; the MGW Pike, the Chambersburg Road and the Furnace Road. This was where both Armies watered their stock after the difficult ascent of South Mountain and they continued as a source of water during the age of early automobiling. the Confederates from the direction of Gettysburg-Fairfield (Fairfield Gap) and the Union troops from the East Emmitsburg (Monterey Gap) These confusing descriptions remained in their reports and minds as a likely landmark for their recollections. Care should be taken in reading and analyzing Monterey Pass material as to which Monterey Springs is actually referenced.

The Confederate train had been laboring up the mountain, through the steep and treacherous Fairfield Gap, the western road to Monterey. Throughout that stormy afternoon, it had been troubled by pounding rain and howling wind that had slashed them with sheets of water. The horses and mules were frightened by the lightning and thunder and became entangled, stubborn and intractable. The wind and dashing rain made it so noisy that even shouted orders and the curses of the teamsters could barely be heard. Small rivulets became roiling torrents. The roads had become washed out seas of mud.

On a collision course with this Confederate train, the Union column continued on and was about to gain the summit of the pass (Monterey). The road was narrow, slippery and crossed with a wide stream, which was normally a trickle. The roadside ditches were filled. It had been pouring since noontime. It was now about 10 o'clock at night and in the midst of a driving thunderstorm, complete with blinding flashes of lightning accompanied and horrific claps of thunder. There was an over-hanging rock precipice on their right and a sheer chasm void to their left. This allowed them scarcely room to move any direction but forward with no space at all to turn a horse or an artillery piece and caisson. The "Boys from Michigan" were between a rock and a hard place. To top it all off, the handicap of their not being able to hear was compounded by their not being able to see more than a foot or two in front of them!

Suddenly, they met with opposition from the heights at Monterey. All that could be heard or seen were the flashes of muskets and the horrendous roar of an artillery piece mixed with the rolling thunder. The horsemen made a strategic withdrawal falling, slipping, sliding over one another, panic stricken, back the way they had come toward Fountaindale, a distance of several hundred yards, to where their Horse Artillery had been deployed.

They regrouped instinctively and charged the heights, reaching the summit within less than fifteen minutes. One of the things that made Kilpatrick's Division so successful was his faith in his young leadership and the stability of his chain of command. His was a close knit unit. It would seem that Halleck's and Meade's philosophy of military re-organization was working.

When they had gained the heights the only thing they could do was return fire at muzzle flashes through the inky darkness. All the way, they were met with the opposition musket fire of ten or twenty infantrymen and a second blast of canister from the Napoleon gun that guarded the roadway. In the throat of the main part of the gap, there was a small plateau of farm fields belonging to Margaret Zeilinger and William Benchoof. The Michigan troops fanned out across these fields and drove the enemy back, strictly with their nerve and numbers. Trowbridge's letter mentioned, "You will perhaps remember that there was a large space of cleared land about a large hotel there." This is where the Battle of Monterey Pass began, near where the open fields and the present rail line cross the Old Baltimore Pike (Now Charmian Road). About where the old watering trough now stands.

"Toward midnight we were nearing the top, marching along a

Antietam Ancestors - Summer Issue - 1989

Monterey Pass

An 1890 view of the Monterey Pass showing the Zeilinger farmhouse (center left) Benchoff homestead (left hand bldg. in upper line of three), Montana Springs Hotel (center) and barn (right). Road is the WGM or Baltimore Pike crossing the B & H Div. of the W.M. Railway that had been opened to Gettysburg in 1889 This was the scene of the lively skirmish and cannonading the dark night of July 4th 1863.

narrow defile, the mountain towering to the right and sloping off abruptly to the left, when the boom of a cannon announced that the advanced guard had encountered the enemy. The piece of artillery was planted in the road, at the summit, near the Monterey House and was supported by the Confederate rearguard which at once opened fire with their carbines. It was too dark to distinguish objects at any distance. The enemy was across the front and no one could tell how large a force it might be. The First Michigan had been sent to the right early in the evening, to attack a body of the enemy hovering on the right flank in the direction of the Fairfield (road) and had a hard fight in which Captain Elliott and Lieutenant McElhenny, two brave officers, were killed. The Fifth and Sixth were leading and at once dismounted and deployed as skirmishers. Generals Kilpatrick and Custer rode to the place where the line was forming and superintended the movement. The Sixth under Colonel Gray was on the right of the line, the road to its left. At least, the portion of the regiment to which my troop belonged was in that position. I think, perhaps, part of the regiment was across the road. The Fifth formed on the left; the First and Seventh in reserve mounted. There is a good deal of guess work about it, for in the darkness one could not tell what was happening except in his immediate neighborhood.

"The order "Forward" finally came and the line of skirmishers advanced up the slope, a column of mounted men following in the road, ready to charge when the opportunity offered. Soon we encountered the Confederate skirmishers, but, could only locate them by the flashes of their guns. The darkness was intense and in a few moments we had plunged into a dense thicket, full of undergrowth, interlaced with vines and briars, so thick that it was difficult to make headway at all. More than once a trailing vine tripped me up and I fell headlong. To keep an alignment was out of the question. One had to be guided by sound and not by sight. The force in front did not appear formidable in numbers, but had the advantage of position and was on the defensive in a narrow mountain pass where numbers were of little avail. We had a large force, but it was strung out in a long column for miles back and it was possible to bring only a few men into actual contact with the enemy, whatever he might be. This last was a matter of conjecture and Kilpatrick doubtless felt the necessity (sic) of moving cautiously, feeling his way until he developed what was in his front. To the right of the road had it not been for the noise and the flashing of the enemy's fire we should have wandered away in the darkness and been lost.

"The Confederate skirmishers were driven back across a swollen stream (Red Run near Monterey Springs) spanned by a bridge. The crossing at this point (nearing the tollgate house and retreating train) was contested fiercely, but portions of the Fifth and Sixth finally forced it and then the whole command crossed over.

"In the meantime, the rumbling of wagon wheels could be heard in the road leading down the mountain. It was evident that we were being detained by a small force striving to hold us there while the train made its escape. A regiment was ordered up mounted to make a charge. I heard the Colonel giving his orders, 'Men,' he said, 'use the saber only; I will cut down any man who fires a shot.' This was to prevent shooting our own men in the melee and in the darkness. Inquiring, I learned it was the First West Virginia Cavalry. This regiment which belonged to the First (Michigan) Brigade had been ordered to report to Custer. At the word, the gallant regiment rushed like the wind down the mountain road, 'yelling like troopers' as they were and good ones, too, capturing everything in their way.

"This charge ended the fighting for that night. It was one of the most exciting engagements we ever had for while the actual number engaged was small and the casualties were not great, the time, the place, the circumstances, the darkness, the uncertainty all combined to make 'the midnight fight at Monterey one of unique interest.' "[17]

The official report of Capt. L Seibert, A.A.G. 1st Brigade, 3rd Division reporting for Major Chas. E. Capehart, Commander of the 1st W. VA Cavalry in command of Farnsworth's Regiment best tells the story of the advance and approach to Monterey Pass:

"We moved up through a mountain gap to Monterey Springs, where quite a body of the enemy were found guarding a wagon train. The Second Brigade (General Custer) had been deployed a (sic – as) skirmishers and had engaged them (the enemy) for an hour when Major Capehart received an order to report with his regiment to General Kilpatrick then at the Monterey House. On doing so, General Kilpatrick ordered him to report to General Custer, he (Major Capehart) was ordered to charge upon the wagon train and, if possible, take it. Major Capehart immediately informed his officers and men of the duty which devolved on them. The charge was ordered and with a whoop and a yell, the regiment dashed down upon the train. The night was one of inky darkness; nothing was

---

17 Kidd, J.H., 1983 (1908) Personal Recollections of a Cavalryman with Custer's Michigan Cavalry Brigade in the Civil War, Collectors Civil War Library, (Alexandria, VA) Time-Life Books.

discernible a half dozen paces ahead. As the advance came up to the train, they received a heavy volley of musketry, which at once showed the exact position of the enemy. Onward they dashed and a hand to hand conflict ensued. The scene was wild and desolating. The road lay down a mountainside, wild and rugged. On either side of the road was a heavy growth of underbrush, which the enemy had taken as fit to conceal themselves and fire upon us. The road was interspersed with wagons and ambulances for a distance of 8 miles and the whole train was taken—300 wagons, 15 ambulances, together all the horses and mules attached. The number of prisoners taken was 1300, including 200 commissioned officers. The casualties of this regiment were two killed and 2 wounded.[18]

It was in this narrow defile where the lane to the Benchoof and Zeilinger farms was that a small force of Confederate Infantry under the command of Captain George M. Emack of Company B of the 1st Maryland Cavalry CSA along with one 12 pound Napoleon gun of the Courtney Henrico Co., Virginia Artillery under the command of Captain W. A. Tanner had been dispatched to defend the summit of the Monterey Pass.

In Capt. Tanner's own words,

"After arriving at the intersection of the

---

18 O.R. Chap.27, Series 1, (Part I) p. 1019, Report of Major Charles E. Capehart, 1st West Virginia.

Emmitsburg Pike and the Millerstown (Old Furnace) Road, I took one of my pieces, with five rounds of ammunition and proceeded to Monterey Springs (hotel), to resist an attack from the enemy upon the wagon train and there remained until about 8 p.m. when the enemy made their appearance. After firing 3 rounds of canister, I repulsed them and fell back about 200 yards and there remained until the enemy made the second advance when I was ordered by General (William E.) Jones to change my position again and withdrew about 100 yards to the rear, where I occupied the third position, when the enemy flanked me both on my right and left and I again canistered them and retired (for want of ammunition in the direction of Williamsport..."[19]

Emack was, but his men were not, aware that they were facing an entire Federal Division: lock, stock and barrel; cavalry, artillery and infantry. This small force delayed the advance of Kilpatrick's Division even though the artillery piece had been withdrawn to the vicinity of the tollhouse, it being low on ammunition. Emack seeing that his small company of men could not hold this large force for very long, recalled his pickets and concealed them in the brush along the sides of the Turnpike and quickly rode back to Monterey Springs and sounded the alarm that the Yankees were advancing on the Headquarters and on the troops bivouacked

---

19 O.R. Chap 27, Series 1, (Part II) p. 498, Report of Capt. W. A Tanner. Courtney (VA) Artillery..

along the road. He continued on westward to the tollhouse to alert Ewell's wagon train to hold their progress onto the Baltimore Pike and to stay hidden on the Furnace Road to avoid the approaching danger. This cleared the road and the forward part of the train moved quickly on toward Buena Vista Springs and Waterloo. This quick thinking on the part of Emack also gained him some reinforcements from Gen. W.E. Jones, who insisted that Ewell's train must move onward toward Williamsport.

CHAPTER FOUR

Miss Hetty and the Farmer's Boy

At the Monterey Springs Hotel, the Confederate headquarters, lately vacated by Captain Emack's alarm (the Confederates had held the Hotel as headquarters and all its occupants as prisoners for 18 hours, its fields the NE corner of the Confederate bivouac, where the ground still held the warmth of sleeping bodies and smoldering campfires) "and there remained until the enemy made a second advance when I was ordered by General [William E.] Jones to change my position again and withdrew about 100 yards to the rear..." (The position of this second withdrawal was at or near the slope that faces toward Monterey at the tollhouse) where I occupied the third position, when the enemy flanked me both on my right and left and I again canistered them and retired (for want of ammunition) in the direction of Williamsport).[1]

The Official Report of General Kilpatrick of August 10, 1863, tells his story:

"We reached Emmitsburg at 3 p.m. Colonel Huey's brigade joined the division at this place. Without halting passed out on the road to Monterey, intending to cross the mountain at that point. Stuart's cavalry was at Miller's. (Millerstown Road) We forced him off the road and passed on. The top of the mountain had nearly been gained when the enemy opened on the advance with artillery and infantry. At the same time, the rear, under Colonel Huey, was attacked by Stuart's Cavalry. On my left was a deep ravine, on my right a steep rugged mountain and a road too narrow to reverse even a gun. To add to this unpleasant position, it was raining in torrents.

"Never under such perilous circumstances did a command behave better; not a word was spoken; there was no confusion. From a farmer's boy[2] I learned the nature of the road and country on the mountain, made

---

1   I O.R. Chap 27, Series 1, (Part II) p. 498, Report of Capt. W. A Tanner. Courtney (VA) Artillery.

2   1860 U.S. Census, Liberty Twp., Adams County, PA, RollM653-1057, Pg. 377, Image 380.
1870 U.S. Census, Liberty Twp., Adams County, PA, RollM593-1289, Pg. 249, Image 498.
History of Franklin County, Warner and Beers, Evansville, Ind. 1887.
The "farmer's boy" referred to by Kilpatrick was Charles H. Buhrman, a 26 year married farmer, who had a wife and two children and employed two (2) hired men on his extensive acreage, just east of the Monterey Pass. He was born June 1,

my disposition and ordered a charge. In a moment, the heights were gained and many prisoners taken. Now the rumble of the enemy's train could be heard rolling down the mountain. The enemy was in position a half a mile farther, at the intersection of the Gettysburg to Hagerstown Turnpike and the road upon which I was moving. The enemy's infantry and artillery were approaching rapidly on the Gettysburg Road and he had already opened on my position with two (?) guns. No time was to be lost if I wished to reach the train and save my command. Pennington, always ready, always willing, quickly came into position and returned the enemy's fire. General Custer's brigade was ordered to move forward, clear the road, and attack the train. The attack was successful.

In the meantime, the First Vermont Cavalry (Lieutenant Colonel Preston) had been sent along the mountain over a wood road to Smithsburg (guided by a farmer's boy) and thence to Hagerstown to intercept the train.

A strong force of dismounted men and two guns of Pennington's battery were now sent on the road in the direction of Gettysburg to barricade the road and hold

---

1837 in Frederick Co., MD. He owned a general store near the Adams/Franklin County line and was to become the owner of the Monterey Springs Hotel and a general store and P.O. in Rouzerville, PA. Note: This "farmer's boy" also was the guide to Preston's 1st Vermont Cavalry over the back mountain road to Smithsburg that dark and stormy night of July 4th, 1863.

the enemy in check until the column had passed. Many a fierce but unsuccessful attacks were made on this position during the night.

At daylight, the whole command had safely passed and Ewell's train was entirely destroyed, save eight forges, thirty wagons and a few ambulances loaded with wounded rebel officers (sent) with the prisoners to Frederick City). At 9 a.m. on the Fifth, the command reached Smithsburg with 1360 prisoners, one battle flag and a large number of horses and mules, several hundred of the enemies wounded being left upon the field."[3]

The firsthand account of the above adventure of Charles H. Buhrman, the "farmer's boy" is given herewith in the form his own firsthand account in a letter addressed to Professor J. Fraise Richard, published by Warner and Beers in 1887 in Chicago, Illinois:

"ROUZERVILLE, PENN. October 12, 1886

MR. J. FRAISE RICHARD,

Dear Sir, Your favor of the 11th inst. Received and questions answered as far as I can remember. I lived at that time at Fountain Dale, Adams Co., Penn. Two miles east of Monterey Springs (Hotel), on the turnpike leading to Emmitsburg. I found out through a man named James Embley, who came to my place and told me that Lee's wagon train was retreating by way of the

---

3   O.R. Series 1, (Part 1,) pg. 993-994.

Old Furnace Road, a mountain road leading from Maria Furnace to the turnpike, coming on the pike near Monterey Springs. "That was on Saturday afternoon, July 4, 1863 as near as I can remember.

"When I found out that Lee's wagon train was retreating, I mounted a horse and started to inform our cavalry, which I supposed would be at Emmitsburg. But two miles below my place, I came to the Yankee pickets and with them was one of Kilpatrick's scouts that I was well acquainted with. I told him of the wagon train retreating; he sent me to Gen. Custer and Custer sent me to Gen. Kilpatrick, At that time, they were just planting a cannon to shell the rebels on McMullan's Hill.

"When I informed Gen. Kilpatrick he ordered an advance at once to Monterey. I rode with the General as far as my farm, two miles east of Monterey. Just before getting to my place we met a little girl that had just left Monterey. She knew me and told me to tell the soldiers not to go to Monterey, as the rebels had planted the pike full of cannons in front of Monterey and would kill all the soldiers when they get there. Kilpatrick laughed and remarked that they kept no account of cannons, as they just rode over them. When I got to the gate that goes into my farm I told the General I lived there and would stop but he requested me to go with them to Monterey and see the fun; so I went with him. We ran against the rebel pickets at Clermont, a quarter of a mile east of Monterey. It was then getting dark in the evening. After passing Clermont about 150 yards the rebels fired three or four shot with grape and canister and then pulled up their battery and retreated. I don't think they killed any of Kilpatrick's men with the battery, as they fired too soon and the grape and canister went over our men's heads; but it made some of our men retreat and caused a great deal of confusion. I told Kilpatrick if he would dismount a regiment and go down through the edge of the woods, he could flank them and capture the battery. He did so but they had retreated by the time our men got to Monterey.

"Kilpatrick asked me which way I thought the wagon train was going and where I supposed they would strike the river. I told him they could go by Smithsburg and Boonsboro and cross the river at Sharpsburg or go by Leitersburg and Hagerstown and cross at Williamsport. He asked me if there was any road that I knew of that I could take a regiment and head off that wagon train. I told him there was, that I could take them by Mount Zion and then down the Raven Rock Hollow and strike Smithsburg and if they had not taken that road, we could cross to Leitersburg and there we would strike them for certain.

It was the 1st Vermont regiment commanded by

Colonel Preston that I was with. When we got to Smithsburg, we found everything quiet, as the rebels had taken the Leitersburg Road. The Colonel asked what was to be done now, as there was no rebels there. I told him we would find plenty of them before daylight, as we must strike them before Leitersburg. We got to Leitersburg about daybreak (July 5th) Sunday morning, finding the road crowded with Rebels, cattle, horses, wagons, etc.

"The regiment I was with captured a great many prisoners, cattle, horses, etc. and destroyed the wagon train from Leitersburg back to Ringgold. There they met the remainder of Kilpatrick's cavalry. They had destroyed the wagon train from Monterey to Ringgold, a distance of six miles and from Ringgold to Leitersburg. A distance of three miles more, making nine miles of wagon train captured, burned or destroyed by cutting off wagon tongues and cutting spokes in wheels. I am not able to say how much, if any, of the wagon train was destroyed between Leitersburg and Hagerstown. As I went only as far as Leitersburg with the 1st Vermont regiment, when it divided, part going toward Hagerstown and part toward Ringgold I went with the part that went toward Ringgold, as that was my way home. I left them at 8 o'clock on Sunday morning and started home by way of Ringgold.

Before I got to Ringgold, I was taken by Kilpatrick's pickets. They took me for a Rebel and all I could say would not change their opinion, as they would not believe anything I said. They took me to the schoolhouse at Ringgold, where the officers had their headquarters; but, as soon as the officers saw me they recognized me, having seen me with Kilpatrick the evening before. After leaving Ringgold, on my way home, on going up a hill near the farm of George Harbaugh, [the farm surrounding present Harbaugh's Church, the hill apparently on the Harbaugh Church Road, north of its intersection with the Pen Mar Road] when I got to the top of the hill the Rebels were coming up the other side. I saw them when I was about 100 yards from them; turned my horse and rode slowly until I got down the hill far enough that they could not see me. Then I ran my horse to the foot of the hill and left the road and got in the woods and got away from them. I kept the woods until I came to the Germantown Road, near the Germantown Schoolhouse; then took a near cut through the swamp and came out on the Sabillasville Road near Monterey, but the Rebel pickets were stationed near Monterey at the turn of the lane.[4] They saw me first and had dis-

4   This is at variance with other descriptions of the occupation of the CSA of Monterey Springs Hotel but it coincides with the description and time of General Lee's arrival at the hostelry and his conference with Gen. Longstreet and Colonel Fairfax, who was taking oaths and issuing Union Soldiers paroles at that place.

mounted and gone around the turn in the lane. I could not see them for a very large cherry tree that stood at the corner of the lane. They let me ride up within about sixty yards of them, when four of them stepped around the turn of the lane and told me to halt. There was an orchard on the left side of the road and a high post fence on each side, I knew my horse could not jump the fence and I did not dare to turn him and go back, as it was a straight lane for a quarter of a mile and they would have easily hit me if I had made the attempt. One of them called for me to dismount and as I was near the orchard fence, I "dismounted" over the fence and did some good running from that to the Pine Swamp about one-fourth of a mile. They shot four times at me, but missed me. I heard balls whistle over my head, as it was downhill and they shot over me. I lost my horse, saddle and bridle. I was in the swamp only a few minutes until they were there; but as the bushes were very thick, I soon got away from them and kept the woods until I got home two miles from there. It was then two or three o'clock on Sunday afternoon. I was at home only a few minutes when I saw the Rebel cavalry coming to my house. They took a near cut from Clermont and came down the old road. They saw me at the same time I saw them. I passed in my front door and out my back door.

"My orchard runs right back of my house and one

of my horses was standing under an apple tree near the house. I mounted the horse and got to the mountain before they were aware that I was not in the house. They searched the house from garret to cellar and told my wife if they found me they would hang me from the first tree they came to. When I got to the mountain, I made a halter out of hickory bark and saved the horse in that way, as they did not find him, I kept myself hid until after the retreat of Lee's army, but lost three horses and nine head of cattle by being away. I have given you the facts as near as I can remember.

Yours very respectfully.

C. H. BUHRMAN"[5]

We are indeed lucky that this first-hand account of a successful local businessman and farmer has been so astutely preserved. It is obvious the C.H. Buhrman was not only a successful man, but, a literate one at that, to give such an account from memory, more than a decade after the fact speaks well of him as well as for his qualities of duty and patriotism.

Another first-hand account of the conditions at the Monterey Springs Hotel, under the Confederate occupation is given in a letter by David Miller, Jr. the manager of the establishment, during this time, prior to his building the competing Clermont[6] Hotel a

5   History of Franklin County, Etc., Bates and Richard, Chicago, Ill. 1887, p. 379ff.
6   The Clermont was the name of Henry Gordon's farm. It was adapted by David Miller for the name of his hostelry when he had left as manager of the Monterey Springs Hotel and built a new hotel on land purchased from Henry Gordon in 1866.

little farther east along the turnpike. He wrote this letter to Prof. J. Fraise Richard, who at the time, along with Samuel P. Bates was gathering material for published history of Franklin County, PA. Miller's account is as follows:

"Clermont, Penn. November 23, 1886

Prof. J. Fraise Richard

Dear Sir – In answer to your letter concerning the capture of Lee's wagon train by Gen. Kilpatrick on the night of July 4 and morning of the 5th 1863, I beg to say I remember it very distinctly.

My father rented Monterey Springs from Mr. Samuel Buhrman and kept the house from April, 1861 to April 1866. Monterey being on the turnpike, at the top of South Mountain is main crossing in the southeastern part of Franklin County, Penn. and was resorted to in times of rebel invasions by not only many persons of Washington and Antrim Townships of this county, but, by many from Washington County, Maryland and the Valley of Virginia. At this place, in times of danger, pickets were always placed from the Monterey House to the western side of the mountain to give notice if the rebels were approaching.

At the times of the Battle of Gettysburg a large number of people were here anxiously awaiting news from the field of carnage, which could be seen from the adjacent hills. On the afternoon of July 4, a company of rebel cavalry came to Monterey from the tollgate, about a half a mile on the western side, where the old Furnace Road intersects the turnpike, over which roads the train was passing. After staying an hour or longer they left and soon a rebel battery came from the same direction and placed a cannon on the turnpike between the house and the barn. Another party was stationed farther east where the Clermont House now is and the pike commences to descend the mountain.

"They kept all the persons at the Monterey as prisoners, placing a guard over them at the house. They gave my nephew, Willie Waddell and myself privilege to go wherever we wished, to look after things, but required us to report every fifteen minutes to Sergt. Grabill, who was stationed at the front door of the house. About dusk, I saw a great deal of commotion among them and asked some of the soldiers what was going on. "Oh, nothing! Just you report to Sergt. Grabill." was the reply. I came to the house and asked Willie Waddell whether he knew what was going on. "Yes." Said he. "I just came down from the observatory on the top of the house and could hear the Union troops coming up the mountain."

"Very soon the cannonading commenced, but did not last long. The rebels hitched horses to their cannon and went toward the tollgate on a run. Sergt. Grabill not waiting for anyone to report to him. One of the first men I met after the arrival of the Union troops was

Gen. Custer, who, after questioning me, called Gen. Kilpatrick standing near. Gen Kilpatrick asked me the distance to the foot of the mountain on the western side and whether troops could march on both sides of the turnpike. I told him they could as far as the tollgate. He immediately ordered a cannon to be placed in front of the Monterey house to throw shells after the retreating rebels. At the same time, he ordered a regiment to march after them. The officer in command said he could not go while they were throwing shells in the rear of his men. Kilpatrick said, "Yes you can." And at the same time directed the officer in charge of the cannon to throw his shells high so that there would be no danger to in the Union troops. The rebels returned the fire from the neighborhood of the tollgate, but, when the Union troops approached they ceased.

"Kilpatrick inquired of me whether there was any other road by which he could get to the foot of the mountain. I informed him of the Mount Zion road to Smithsburg and Leitersburg, the distance to the former place being eight miles, to the latter eleven. He then asked me if I knew any one acquainted with the road who would go as a guide. I had seen Mr. C.H. Buhrman with the soldiers when they came to Monterey. I said, "Mr. Buhrman is the man for you." Mr. Buhrman being called up, Gen. Kilpatrick asked him whether he knew the Mount Zion road to Smithsburg and Leitersburg, and asked him whether he could find it on such a dark night, if so, whether he would go as guide for a regiment. Mr. Buhrman said he knew the road well, could find it no matter how dark the night, and would go as guide.

"Calling Col. Preston, Gen Kilpatrick informed him that Mr. Buhrman would act as his guide. Soon the tramping of horses began through the mud and rain in one of the darkest nights I ever knew. As soon as Col. Preston had started, Gen. Kilpatrick ordered a lieutenant with James McCulloh as guide to go past the Benchoff farm to the old Furnace road to cut off that portion of the train between the Gum Spring and the turnpike, which added one and a half miles more to the part already attacked and from which they brought from seventy-five to one hundred prisoners to Monterey. The cannonading continued for several hours as our troops were descending the western side of the mountain. By day light on Sunday morning, July 5, Gen. Kilpatrick, with all his troops and prisoners except a few who were too badly wounded to be moved, had left Monterey. One of these wounded died soon after.

"I never knew any one to direct movement as rapidly as Gen. Kilpatrick did that night, nor men so eager to follow as were the Union soldiers. There never was a greater victory under such adverse circumstances with the loss of so small a number of men.

Respectfully yours,

DAVID MILLER"[7]

David Miller's account of the interception of the Confederate train bears out the legend of Henrietta "Hetty" Zeilinger who was mentioned previously by C. H. Buhrman's account when he accompanied Kilpatrick's troops as they stormed the heights of Monterey.

Hetty Zeilinger was the seventeen year old daughter of the widowed (female) farmer Margaret Zeilinger, widow of George A. Zeilinger who along with William Benchoff owned farmland in the wide plateau that was the opening to the pass at Monterey. These farms lie along the east side of the railroad and extend northward toward Old Furnace Road.[8]

As the Michigan Cavalry was deployed to cut off the retreating Confederate wagon train, they fell in with the young girl whose farm they were crossing and she consented, over the objections of her mother and sisters, Elizabeth and Margaret, to guide them through the dense forest to the Gum Spring and the moving train. Hetty took them past the Benchoff barn, through the fields and along a narrow path in the woods and pointed them in the direction of the Furnace Road, this, despite the roaring thunderstorm and dashing rain that was in progress.

Several soldiers of the 1st Michigan Cavalry, later wrote her letters after they reached bivouac quarters in the Valley of Virginia:

---

7   History of Franklin County, etc. Bates and Richard, Chicago, Ill. 1887, p. 381ff.
8   See U.S. Census on Microfilm 1860, Pennsylvania, Washington Twp, Franklin Co. 4 July 1860, Pg. 958.

"Upperville, VA   July 21, 1863

Miss Hetty Zeilinger

"Although I never saw your face to describe your appearance and personal looks but I know well you (sic) character and disposition. The act of guiding me and my party down the side of the mountain that dark night, down that dark lane, across those creeks, alone, among rough and strange soldiers is enough to convince me of the nobleness of your character, magnamity of soul and the staunchest loyalty to our country.

"Hetty, I cannot help but admire you. I beg pardon for the expression. There were several of our boys wounded that night and four or five missing and some that were wounded at Fairfield were carried to the Monterey house. I believe you live close by there or at least it was not far from there where we found you or you found us. One Corporal Shanahan was wounded in the leg and has since had the limb amputated. It would give me pleasure to hear that you visited them (sic). Two men of my company, Corporal Rich and William Simons have not been seen or heard from since that night, they are both of my Co. and were by my side at the discharge of grape and canister. We stayed around that hill that morning until about 2 o'clock and pushed on. We have had very hard times since then.

We done a good deal of hard fighting around

Hagerstown, Boonsboro and Williamsport and wound up at Falling Waters, where we had the sharpest fight I think we ever had. Our Cav. Brigade was in pursuit of a Division of Infantry and we overtook them and killed or took prisoners more than our own no.(number) and we lost only a few men. We went up to Ashby Gap yesterday and expected to have a fight but the Rebs, seeing our disposition of men evacuated without firing a shot. We are laying here resting today.

Hetty

Please write me Direct to

Lieut. A.E. Matthews

Co. H. 1st Michigan Cav

Washington, D.C.

I am obliged, Yours etc.

A. E. Matthews (s)"

"To Miss Hetty

On the Mountain"

"P.S. If you see the boys at Monterey House please inform them that you have heard from me and oblige AEM(s)"[9]

Miss Hetty was much admired by the boys from Michigan. One can't be sure of the reason. Perhaps it was for her pluck, perhaps her looks, perhaps her age and vulnerability. We'll never know whether she sought out the wounded soldiers at the

---

9   Cursive Letter in the original; Courtesy of the late John Krebs Benchoff

Monterey House or answered their letters. She eventually married Jacob Fitz, a local farmer and lived in a house he built, in close proximity to her mother, Margaret, who died in 1891 and is buried in the Fountaindale, (PA) Union Cemetery.

The second letter is as follows:

"Camp Near Warrenton Junction, VA

August 7, 1863

Please excuse these fiew(sic) lines

From a Friend

"You will excuse me for taking this liberty but I thought I would write a fiew(sic) lines to let you know where I was. I suppose you remember the night of the 4th of July when you guided a squad of the 1st Michigan Cavalry around in those mountains(sic) and showed them the way to the main road. I was among that squad & as you gave me your naim(sic) & Post office address I thought while I had the opportunity I would improve it in writing to you. I am well as usual & when this reaches you I hope it will find you the same. I can tell you we have had very busy times since we was on the mountain there. We was engaged at the battle of Boonesborough & at Hagerstown & at Falling Waters we had two men killed and several wounded at the latter place. We have had but one skirmish since we came to this State. The Army is laying still now it seames(sic) we are recruiting our horses here they was all pretty well used up when we first stoped(sic) here but I think we will soon have them fit for sirvis(sic) again. but I am in hopes they will end this war without much more fiting(sic) for my part I am getting tired of it & I think the rebs are as willing to have it ended as we ar(sic) & perhapse(sic) more so, all the prisoners that we have taken say they ar(sic) glad that they was taken & in hopes(sic) we would capture there(sic)whole Army which we could have dun(sic) iff(sic) our Army had atacted(sic) them two days before they did at Hagerstown & Williamsport.

"I don't know as I can think of any thing more that will bee(sic) very interesting. So I will bring this to a close. Iff(sic) you think this worth answering I should be very happy to here(sic) from you. My best respects (to) & well wishes to you.

Yours very respectfully

Franklin Huff (s)

Direct to the

1st Michigan Cavalry

Company M

Washington, D.C.

Please excuse the bad writing and spelling"[10]

There are several other local accounts of the engagement at Monterey Pass and one of the most colorful was related by Dr. Henry G. Chritzman, a local Welsh Run (PA) physician and staunch Unionist that early in the war was appointed a civilian

---

10 Cursive Letter in the original; Courtesy of the late John Krebs Benchoff.

contract surgeon, later was commissioned as an Assistant Surgeon and in 1864 was commissioned a Surgeon with the rank of Major attached to Colonel Pennock Huey's 2nd Brigade of Brigadier General D. M. Gregg's cavalry division. He practiced medicine in the Mercersburg vicinity until his death in 1909. He was a graduate of the Pennsylvania Medical College; President of the Pennsylvania Medical Society and served two terms in the Pennsylvania Legislature.[11] He had served as Surgeon in the 101st Regiment of the PA. Vol. Infantry from 14th December 1861 until his muster out on 4 February 1863 and then as Ass't. Surgeon in the 87th Regiment of the PA Cavalry from 14 March 1863 until the expiration of his term on 11 October, 1864.

The author of these poetic lines aside from Sir Walter Scott, is not at all clear but all signs point to it being written by either Colonel Huey or Dr. Chritzman:

"July 4th we moved to Emmitsburg and reported to Kilpatrick; moved the same evening to intercept Ewell's wagon train which was reported to be near Monterey Springs. The brigade moved rapidly up the mountain road striking Ewell's train about 3 o'clock in the morning of July 5th, in the midst of a furious thunderstorm, whilst on its retreat from Gettysburg. Quoting Sir Walter Scott:

'At once there rose so wild a yell
Within that dark and narrow dell
As if all the fiends from heaven that fell,
Had pealed the banner cry of hell.'

---

11   Thrush, Ambrose Wells, MD, <u>Medical Men of Franklin Co. (PA) 1750-1925,</u> Chambersburg, PA. Medical Society of Franklin County, p. 369.

"This combined with the Plutonic darkness made it one of the nights long to be remembered. When we came up with the wagon train, Federal and Confederate cavalry, wagons ambulances, drivers and mules became a confused mass of pursued and pursuing demons whose shouts and carbine shots mingled with the lightning's red glare and the thunder's crash, made it appear as if we were in the infernal regions especially so as the cries of the wounded often rose high above the din of conflicting forces.

"Frequently a driver would be shot or leave his mule team, when the unrestrained animals would rush wildly down the narrow road and in many instances the wagons with the mules attached would be found at daylight at the bottom of some deep ravine crushed to pieces with the mules dead or dying. It was a fearful ride suiting well the fearless intrepidity of out daring commander.

"A Confederate brigade, then a long train of wagons and ambulances, then our brigade in the center, with Ewell's corps in our rear, going down that narrow mountain road upon the principle of the devil take the hindmost—you have Kilpatrick's dash across Monterey Pass.

"The result of this brilliant movement was the capture of a large number of wagons, ambulances and mules with fifteen hundred prisoners. The brigade reached the foot of the mountain about daylight, leaving the Baltimore Pike where it turns toward Waynesboro. The column moved on toward Smithsburg, Maryland where the wagons and ambulances were burning. The command rested at this place during the day. As the shades of evening drew nigh we were treated to a compliment of shot and shell by Stuart, who appeared at Raven Rock Gap above the little village. Soon our battery got into position when Stuart was compelled to retire; our brigade taking up the line of march for Boonsborough, (sic) where it arrived about midnight without further interruption."[12]

Quite a dramatic and poetic description. It's is amazing that all of the recorded descriptions, although at variance in numbers and certain details, generally agree with each other as to times, locale, weather and other detail that is important. To get an idea of the scene of carnage and destruction General Robert E. Lee, Gen. Longstreet and their retinue of staff officers rode into that fateful morning July 5, 1863 from a handwritten daybook by an unknown author attached to the 1st Vermont Cavalry comes this:

"July 5, 1863

On the South Mountain, our div. (division) left the battlefield at 3 o'clk yesterday to cut off part of the rebel trains and capture his artillery. While passing over the mountain last evening, we came upon a rebel train just on top of the mountain. Kilpatrick charged into the rear, capturing the guards, over a "thousand prisoners including Gen. Jones (Gen. Jones was not captured) and burned over three miles of train loaded with every kind of plunder from a woman's petticoat to a mowing

---

12 Hoke, Jacob, The Great Invasion of 1863, Dayton, Ohio, The Otterbein Press, 1913, p.452.

machine. Many of the boys procured a good suit of new clothes from the train. Being very weary and my horse having given out I concluded to get into the nearest barn and sleep, if possible, in my drenched clothes for it had rained ever since we left Gettysburgh (sic). Early the next morning, the lady of the house, a kind Union woman came and waked up all who were in the barn and warned us that the rebels were on picket just a few rods off. This was at the small town of Monterey just on top of the mountain. We proceeded half way down the mountain on the road to Emmitsburgh (sic) and were halted by a citizen who conveyed to us the pleasing intelligence that the rebels held the city in force and our only hopes were to hide in the mountain until our Cavalry should come in and drive them out. This we did and the kind people, never to be forgotten, brought us everything we desired to eat, until toward evening a farmer saddled his horse and riding to the city, found the Rebel Cavalry had left and Col. McIntosh commanding a brig (brigade) of Gregg's Cav. (Cavalry) held the place...I am particularly thankful to Mr. Coffin [Coffelt], living on the mountain, who aiding in secreting several of us endangered his own life."[13]

---

13 GNMP Vertical File 4-14; Manuscript Diary attributed to member of Co "A" 1st Vermont Cavalry.

General Lee after assessing the damage to Ewell's supply train passed the tollgate intersection and proceeded west on the turnpike to the legendary Lee's Rock #2, which is situated about a quarter of a mile toward Hagerstown from the toll house on the south side of the road (See illustration).

Photo by Ryan Smith

Lee's Rock #2

Near mailbox #14079 on Southside Old Routh #16, a short distance south of the Tollhouse on turnpike.

CHAPTER FIVE

Road To Frogtown, Smithsburg and a Barbeque

Before General Lee spoke from this natural platform, his servants had erected a small tent, nearby, which he entered and sat at a small table writing orders and dispatches that directed the withdrawal of troops and their crossing of the Potomac. It was not until he reached Hagerstown on July 7, that he wrote a letter to Jefferson Davis explaining his unsuccessful campaign and complained of the failure of the Union to uphold the parole agreement.[1]

After some time, General Lee emerged, the tent was struck and he climbed up on the legendary Lee's Rock #2 and made "a short

---

1   Dowdey and Manarin, Edit. <u>The Wartime Papers of R.E. Lee</u>, Virginia Civil War Commission, Little Brown & Co., Boston, 1st Edition, 1961. Also: O.R. Series II, Vol. 39, pg. 298-299.

address" to his officers. "A bystander, Samuel Wallace, a hostler, who had an opportunity to hear him, related that he (Lee) spoke very feelingly of his officers and men who had lost their lives on the battlefield, mentioning some of his closest friends by name. He told his officers they must now go back to Virginia and his main concern was to get the wounded men safely on the other side of the River (sic)... It was a significant and gloomy speech, for here, (at this spot) he looked down on the wonderful (beautiful?) Cumberland Valley and gave expression to (his) discouragement."[2]

General Lee mounted Traveller and went onward along the turnpike through the broken down gun carriages, the burned and broken wagons and dead mules toward Waterloo (Rouzerville) and Waynesborough, (Waynesboro) as the villages were then called,[3] he passed the Buena Vista Inn and when he reached Frogtown or Pikesville (as Rouzerville was then called), he took the road leading to Waynesboro and stopped at a tavern, where he and his party sat down to their first properly prepared meal in many days.

If one is to take seriously the accounts of Lee's journey from Monterey to Waynesborough it could be said that he didn't leave

2   Stoner, Jacob H., <u>Historical Papers, Franklin County and the Cumberland valley Pennsylvania</u>; Compiled by his wife, Lucole Stoner, The Craft Press, Chambersburg, PA, 1947, p. 464.

3   Peter Rouzer did not layout the village that bears his name until about 1868 and then it was called Pikesville. Atlas' of the period show Waterloo, which was on the stagecoach route between Hagerstown and Gettysburg. It was shown as the more densely populated village. Rouzerville was not so named until the U. S. Post Office was established there in 1873. (Gordy, U.L. <u>Kittochtinny Historical Papers</u>, Volume 11, p. 5, Chambersburg, PA., 1938)

Pennsylvania ill-fed and that his small group literally ate their way to the river. Up to this time the General and staff had taken a snack of tea and biscuits at the Benchoff Farm (Chapter #1- Lee's Rock #1). Then proceeded to the Monterey House where they had a small repast. In the group had passed the Buena Vista[4] wagon stop on their way down the mountain, but did not stop there perhaps because it was in close proximity to the site of General Lee's last "hastily prepared meal" near the locale of Lee's Rock #2.

4   There are few references to Buena Vista, a wagon stop of longstanding, even to pre-turnpike years, during the Civil war that we can find: 1. A reference to Samuel Wade, an alleged deserter being captured near Buena Vista Springs on March 5, 1863 previously mentioned in Chapter 3. 2. A newspaper reference to a famished Confederate officer being seen near Buena Vista stripping wild cherries from a tree and hungrily devouring them, while still in the saddle. (n.p., n.d.) 3. An article in the (Waynesborough, Pa.) Village Record September18,1863, shortly after the Battle of Gettysburg: "A SOLDIER SHOT AT----- One night last week one of the soldiers from this place (Waynesborough) was shot at on the mountain, near Buena Vista Springs, whilst out on picket duty, the ball passing close to his head. This was a bold attempt at assassination and we trust the copperhead scoundrel who discharged the weapon may yet be found out and receive his just deserts." It was at this time 1863 after the Battle of Gettysburg that there was a great turmoil and agitation over "copperheads," northern sympathizers with the confederacy. They were mostly Democrats and violently opposed to President Lincoln and his policies, particularly the Emancipation Proclamation which they had worked long and hard in Congress to block its adoption. The copperheads were hated by Northern patriots and confrontations between these two factions often became violent and deadly. The central area of these civilian conflicts was in the southern parts of Ohio, Illinois, Indiana and Pennsylvania. The Village Record of Waynesborough, September 18, 1863, "The "copperheads of the North realize the precariousness of their friends (the Confederacy's) situation and are getting weak in the knees. Six or seven months ago it was a common thing for some of this class to cheer for Jeff Davis, Vallandigham or some other prominent traitor and flaunt "copperhead" badges; but this emblem of treason has disappeared and we no longer hear shouts going up for these traitors. They were hopeful then, but Grant, Banks, Meade…and others, whom posterity will bestow the highest medal of honor, have deprived them of this sweet consolation, and hence they are somewhat given to despondency, and promise ere long to become perfectly docile."

When they reached the intersection of the Waynesboro and Hagerstown Pike at the top of the Pikesville hill, Lee and his men made a sharp right turn and headed toward Waynesboro. Perhaps the Hagerstown road was too littered with the debris of the decimated train or too crowded with retreating troops. There was moving traffic everywhere.

Stoner said, "This battle which centered on Rouzerville should have a name. At first thought, it would seem to be appropriate to call it the battle of South Mountain but there was (is) a battle of the Civil War given that name. Possibly it should be called the Battle of Mason and Dixon line as part of the skirmish occurred on both sides of the Mason and Dixon line and there is no other engagement of the Civil War that has the distinction of being fought on both sides of the Mason and Dixon line. It could be called 'The Battle of Rouzerville' but that would not do as the little town was then known as Pikesville."

Stoner exhorts that. "The school children of Franklin County and especially the children of Washington Township on whose soil it was fought should be taught the facts of this battle. There are numerous instances recorded of several generations having passed away before the significance of some event was fully recognized and given its rightful place in history and truly this battle is one of those instances of belated recognition."[5]

This was probably the first such proposal but certainly not the last! In 1954, in a paper read before the Kittochtinny Historical Society of Chambersburg, Franklin County, PA, Dr Frank Bohn

---

5   Stoner, J.H., Op cit, p 464

proposed that a statue be erected upon Lee's Rock #2 in recognition of Lee's influence in bringing the people of the Confederacy back into the Union. Dr. Bohn claimed this consummated the labor and leadership begun by Abraham Lincoln. He asserted that without proper direction our Southland might have become another divided holy land or another Ireland. This historical paper was delivered at the site of Lee's address to his staff and concludes that Robert E. Lee was just as much a hero to the North as he was to the South.[6]

The citizens of Pikesville said that the advance of Kilpatrick's cavalry was so swift, and the fighting so brisk, that the sound of the charge, coupled with the thunderstorm, that probably enhanced it, sounded like rolling thunder and the interspersed firing of carbines and muskets made it sound like fireworks that 4th of July night.

Daylight revealed that two Confederate soldiers lay dead near the Hagerstown Turnpike Toll House at the top of Pikesville hill. These two men were buried in the yard of 12128 Old Route 16, the John L. Martin (present Flaugher) house.[7] There seems to be no government census that they were ever disinterred. At

---

6 Bohn, Frank, Ph. D. Kittochtinny Historical Society; *Chambersburg, Franklin County, PA; Papers Read Before the Society, Vol. XIII, Oct, 1950 to May 1957* Thursday Evening, October 28, 1954; p.367
See also, *Public Opinion Newspaper*, Chambersburg, Franklin Co., PA, October 29, 1954. p. 1
Note: Dr. Frank Bohn (1878-1975) was a noted lyceum (which see) speaker and an authority on European history and international affairs, a world traveler and was a pre-*Voice of America/Radio Free Europe* USA propagandist and undercover foreign agent throughout free Europe.

7 Local tradition

Waterloo, the fighting was particularly heavy and two North Carolina soldiers were killed in that vicinity. [8]

For many years after this occurrence there could still be seen along the course of this road broken wheels, spokes, felloes, hubs and other parts of wagons and gun carriages and horse tack—mute evidence of the destruction inflicted on the Confederates by Kilpatrick's cavalry.

All the while, along the Hagerstown Turnpike, toward Ringgold and Smithsburg things were just beginning to heat up. It will be remembered that Gen. J.E.B Stuart had made a bee-line, under orders from General Lee to parallel the course of the retreating Confederates along the east ridge of the Blue Ridge and to keep his cavalry guard between the Federals heading between Washington and Lee's with-drawing troops. What neither Lee nor Stuart had reckoned with had been that Kilpatrick's 1st Vermont and Michigan troops had proceeded them by the same route (Mt Zion Road) and also in their attack on the wagon train by way of Ringgold to arrive at Smithsburg early on the morning of the 5th of July. Custer's 2nd Brigade had succeeded in running down Ewell's wagon train and disabling it as far as Ringgold and on toward Leitersburg.

"The head of this column reached Ringgold at about daylight—the whole command, horses as well as men, tired, hungry, sleepy, wet and covered with mud. Men and animals yielded to the demands of exhausted nature and the column had

---

8   Raiford, Neil Hunter, _The 4th North Carolina in the Civil War,_ McFarland and Co., Jefferson, NC; 2003 and GNMP file _Record of Confederate Burials, The Journal of Dr John W.C. O'Neal, MD,_ p. 40.

not been halted many minutes before all fell asleep where they stood. Under the friendly protection of the dripping eaves of a chapel[9], a gay and gallant brigadier could have been seen, enjoying in the mud, one of those sound sleeps only obtained through fatigue, his long golden locks matted with the soil of Pennsylvania. Near him, in the mud lay a dandyish adjutant, equally oblivious of the toilet, upon which he generally bestowed so much attention. Under the fence near at hand is reclining a well-got-up Major, whose stylish appearance and regular features have turned the heads of many fair damsels on Chestnut Street; here a chaplain, there a trooper, a Commanding General, aids, (sic) orderlies and servants for the nonce meet on the (same) level. The faithful trooper lies by his horse between whom and himself there seems to exist an indescribable community of feeling. Two hours are thus passed in sleep—the provost-guard only on duty—when the word is passed that "that the column is all closed up," which is the signal to move on again. The indefatigable Estes shakes himself and proceeds to shake the Commanding General, to let him know that the object for which the halt was made had been accomplished; that it is time to move. Five minutes more and all are in the saddle again and marching for Smithsburg. A body of armed

---

9   The chapel referred to was the Reverend Christian Frantz' Franzite Mennonite Church which had been built in the property upon which the church was built had the Mason-Dixon line as its south boundary. The church building was in Franklin County, Pennsylvania, while its burial ground to the south of the building lay in Washington County, MD. This church was not used for many years but was used as a farmers tenant house. It was razed in 1922. The consecrated burials were disinterred and moved to Green Hill Cemetery in the Borough of Waynesboro. This action required Court petitions and orders from courts in Maryland and Pennsylvania.

men, mailed in mud! What a picture. Smithsburg was reached by 9 o'clock A.M. The reception they met with there made all forget the trials of the night—made them forget even their fatigue. It was Sunday. The sun shone forth brightly, young girls lined the street-sides, singing patriotic songs; the General was showered with flowers, and troops were cheered until reechoed by the mountain side; young ladies and matrons assailed the column with words of welcome and large plates heaped with pyramids of white bred (sic), spread with jelly and butter, inviting all to partake.[10]

"...The troops prepared to enjoy a quiet Sunday dinner in the small community (Smithsburg) nestling at the foot of the mountain. To this end they had secured...a steer, had slaughtered it and had hung the carcass on a huge elm just south of town, awaiting the right moment when the open pit fires would be ready to transform the raw meat into a delectable feast of barbecued beef. Imagine the consternation and fury engendered in the Union camp when a volley of shot from Stuart's lone cannon on Nicodemus Hill interrupted their happy anticipation of a satisfying Sabbath repast!

"With no appetite for a situation which placed the resourceful Stuart on the heights while the Union soldiers were forced to make a stand in the valley, General Kilpatrick hastily broke camp, left the beef hanging to the old elm and with more "than deliberate speed hastened toward the safety of Hagerstown and the aid of other Union contingents...

---

10 Whittaker, Frederick, A Complete Life of Gen. George Armstrong Custer, University of Nebraska Press, Lincoln, Neb. And London, Reprint 1876, Edition, 1993, p. 184

"After the Confederate forces had passed through Smithsburg, a rifle made in Richmond was found abandoned in a large bank barn on the farm of Thomas A. Brown, in the valley beneath Nicodemus Hill.

"Mute evidence of the engagement described above is found in a cannonball in a brick wall of the then Leonard Vogel house, now the Forrest House at 25 East Water Street, Smithsburg..."[11]

Stuart's approach and the taking of Smithsburg were not quite

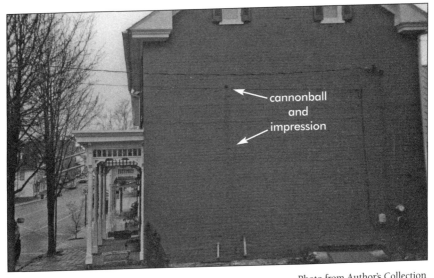

cannonball
and
impression

Cannonball House

A souvenir artifact embedded in the wall of a Smithsburg, MD Water Street house has remained there since July 5, 1863, a reminder that Stuart's Light Artillery was surveying Kilpatrick's celebration barbeque from Nicodemus Hill.

11 Smithsburg, MD Vertical File, Washington County Free Library, Hagerstown, MD. Titled: " This story came to me from my grandfather who was an eyewitness to the Battle of Smithsburg, 5 July 1863" N.p., n.d. See also: Fehl, A. P. Pahmphlet: *Smithsburg and the Civil War*, Smithsburg Historical Society, 1987, n.p.

as straightforward as the foregoing description might intimate. Stuart had started his cavalry toward Frederick after the Battle of Gettysburg with express orders to protect the left flank of Ewell's retreating train.[12]

This account is from Stuart's written report of Chambliss and Jenkins Brigade on the retrograde movement from Gettysburg. The report finds him at Emmitsburg on the Frederick Road at dawn on July 5th 1863:

> "In and around Emmitsburg we captured 60 or 70 prisoners of war and some valuable hospital stores en route from Frederick to the (Union) army.

> "The march was resumed on the road to Frederick till we reached a small village called Cooperstown[13]

---

12 O.R. Series 1, Capter 27, (Part II) p. 699

13 Stuart probably misnamed the settlement that he called "Cooperstown" and a logical explanation for this is stated in a letter written by Frederick Tilberg, Historian of Gettysburg National Military Park, October 30, 1964. Tilberg states, "Marching southward on the road to Frederick, Stuart says that he reached a village called *Cooperstown* where the route selected turned sharply to the right to enter Harbaugh's Valley and then across the mountain...In the Atlas of Frederick County of 1873, Mechanicstown (Thurmont) District #15, *Coopers Sh(op)* is indicated in a line of homes adjacent to the Emmitsburg-Mechanicsville (Thurmont) road three miles north of the latter place according to the scale indicated. It is at that point that the road to Harbaugh's Valley bears sharply to the right. This point, I am reasonably certain, at some stage in pre-war or the war period history, was called Cooperstown. It is so indicated, of course in Stuart's Report." Gettysburg National Miliary Park, Vertical File 4-15.

It is the author's opinion that Tilberg erred here on two points, 1. The atlas denoted a group of buildings occupied by coopers engaged in making flour barrels for nearby mills. 2. The road that bears sharply to the right does not enter Harbaugh's Valley or Eyler's Valley, instead this road follows Owens Creek Valley. The entrance to Harbaugh's Valley topographically lies along a tributary of Friends Creek in Frederick County, MD near Sabillasville at its southern end and terminates near Zora in Adams County, PA and does not come near Mechanicstown (Thurmont). The entrance to Eyler's Valley lies at Emmitsburg, Frederick County, MD for its northern terminus and debauches into Harbaugh's Valley north of Carrick's Knob (College Mt) as its southern end.

where our route turned short to the right. Here I halted the column to feed as the horses were much fatigued and famished. The column after an hour's halt, continued through Harbaugh's Valley, by Zion Church, to pass the Catoctin Mountain. The road separated before debouching from the mountain, one fork leading to the left to Smithtown and the other, to the right, bearing more toward Leitersburg.

"I divided my command, in order to make the passage more certain, Colonel Ferguson commanding Jenkins Brigade taking the left Road and Chambliss Brigade which I accompanied, the other. Before reaching the western entrance to this pass, I found it held by the enemy and had to dismount a large portion of the command, and fight from crag to crag of the mountain to dislodge the enemy, already posted. Our passage was finally forced and as my column emerged from the mountains, it received the fire of the enemy's battery, posted to the left on the road to Boonsborough, I ascertained, too, about this time by the firing that the party on the other route had met with resistance and sent at once to apprise Colonel Ferguson of our passage and directed him, if not already through, to withdraw and come by the same route I had followed. Our artillery was soon in position and a few fires drove the enemy from his position.

"I was told by a citizen that the party I had just

attacked was the cavalry of Kilpatrick, who had claimed to have captured several thousand prisoners and 400 or 500 wagons from our forces near Monterey; but I was further informed that not more than 40 wagons accompanied them and other facts I heard led me to believe the success was overrated. About this time, Captain [G.M.] Emack, Maryland cavalry, with his arm in sling, came to us and reported that he had been in the fight the night before and partially confirmed the statement of the citizen and informed me to my surprise, that a large portion of Ewell's corps trains has preceded the army through the mountains."[14]

An interesting account, given here (in part), was given in <u>A Prisoners March From Gettysburg to Staunton</u> by John L. Collins, 8th Pennsylvania Cavalry: (Collins, as prisoner, marched with Stuart's Brigade as they approached Smithsburg.)

"On the 4th, when Lee's movement of withdrawal became known, the cavalry was ordered to throw itself between the

---

14 *O.R. Series 1, Chapter 27,* (Part II),Report of Gen. J.E.B. Stuart, August 20, 1863. Pp 700-701. It is the author's opinion that here General Stuart erred in his official report and that he and his troops never came close to Harbaugh's Valley. They followed the narrow defile of Owen's Creek Valley past Lantz and westward to its source near Mount Moriah Church *not Zion Church*. Had they reached Harbaugh Valley, Stuart would have <u>certainly</u> mentioned Sabillasville, which was at that time a substantial settlement and this route would have carried him through Skunk Hollow directly to Zion Church; instead Stuart had followed Owens Creek to its source and thence to Mt Moriah Church where the column divided; Stuart (Chambliss Brigade) took the right fork which carried him directly to Raven Rock Hollow via Zion Church and Ferguson (Jenkins Brigade) took the left hand fork in the road which carried him directly to Nicodemus Hill overlooking Smithsburg.

Confederate army and the Potomac. To do this the different divisions were headed for the gaps and passes through which the trains sent under escort in advance were escaping over the mountains to Williamsport.

"The regiment to which I belonged was in Gregg's division, but, having become detached with the rest of the brigade during the three days of battle, it united with the other two brigades under General Kilpatrick and made an attack upon the Confederate train near Monterey. The fight took place before midnight the first day of the march, the train was burned, the guard were made prisoners and then our command pushed on after another train that was reported ahead of the one we destroyed. A few whose horses were killed or disabled were ordered back to the "division for a remount instead of being mounted on the enemy's horses. I disobeyed orders and hoping to get one of the enemy's horses, I led my own and followed on foot. I soon lost sight of the brigade, however, but toiled along the dark and rough road, until my horse, which, at first, could walk with only the weight of the saddle, refused to go any farther. As the day was breaking, I was examining and washing the poor creature's wounded shoulder, when I was surprised by about 150 Confederate cavalry, whose approach I had hailed as friends. At a motion from their colonel, three men dismounted, the foremost of whom held out his hand to me and cheerfully said: "Good morning, sir! I am sorry to say you are a prisoner." The other two went toward my arms, which were piled on the saddle on the roadside and holding them up exclaimed, "What splendid arms he has!" Surprise and the novelty of the first man's greeting kept me from realizing my position until I saw them take my carbine, saber and pistol. Then my heart sank.

"Those "splendid arms" had been my companions for two years and two months previously. I had been publicly commended for bringing them with me through the enemy's ranks when my horse was shot inside their lines as we charged upon Jackson's men at Chancellorsville. But, such is war and I bade them a sorrowful adieu as I looked from them to the faces of my captors, some of which showed sympathy, some indifference, while seemed manly and soldierly. The commander alone took no notice of me or my arms; he gazed up the road through the gray light of the morning as if bent on some bold manoevre (sic) and then said to one of his men in a loud voice, "Tell General Lee, (Fitzhugh) that there is a regiment of Yankee cavalry half a mile up the road and ask him if I shall charge them."

"The man galloped back and without waiting for General Lee's orders, the colonel wheeled his men and galloped after him—such a piece of cheap braggadocio as I had seen displayed by some of my own colonels. I was left in the care of two men to put the saddle on my horse and follow at a walk. My guards were frank and in answer to my question told me that they belonged to General William E. Jones brigade, that they had been captured in the fight just mentioned (Monterey) and had escaped during the night from Kilpatrick who was more intent in overtaking larger bodies than in watching the few hundred he had taken. Between midnight and daybreak the colonel and about 150 men came

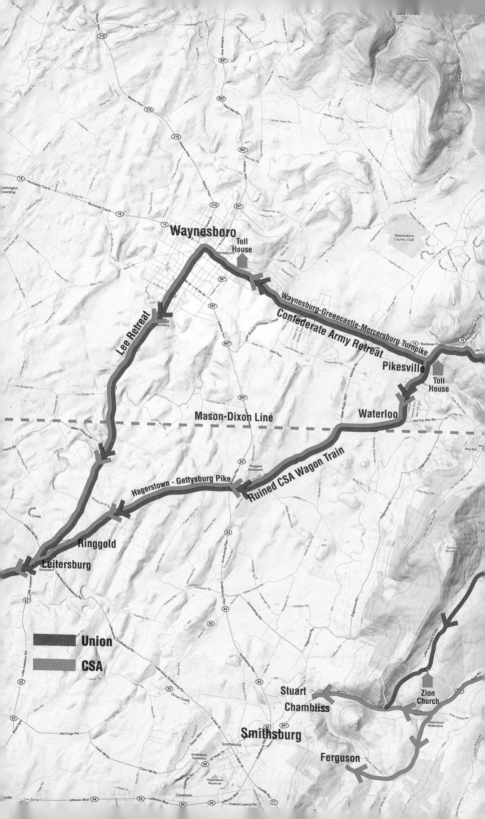

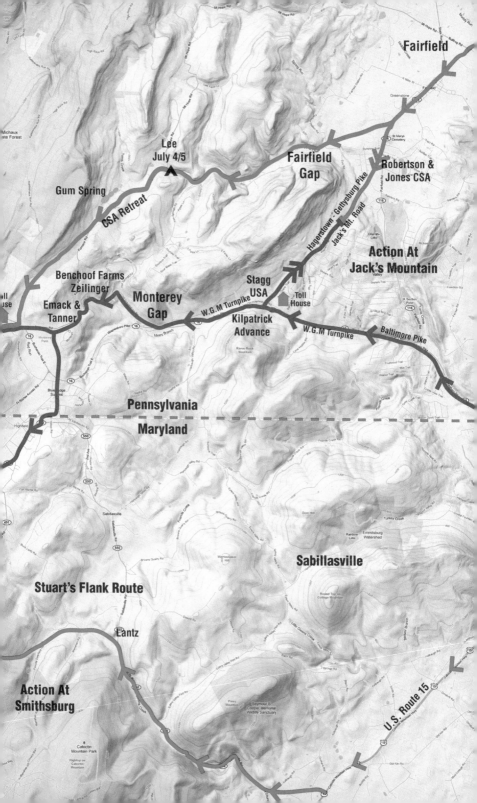

together in the woods and fell in with General Fitzhugh Lee, who was slipping out between two divisions of our cavalry.

"About noon I was introduced to about thirty of those who had been sent back for horses to the division and had shared my fate. We were with General Stuart's headquarters (company) as he was moving in the center of his brigades–they being pushed out in every direction, trying to keep the road clear for their infantry and artillery.

"A young Virginian about my own age, but, with much more suavity and self-complacency than I could claim, introduced himself to me and told me that he belonged to the "King and Queen" cavalry (1st Virginia, I think) and said that they "knew my regiment well and considered it a "rough one to deal with." He asked me "if I remembered all the skirmishes we had as we advanced from New Kent Courthouse to the Chickahominy, which I did well and then when we had become quite well acquainted, asked me if I would have any objections to exchanging saddles with him. I had not the least, as I never expected to sit on mine again and when stopped on the roadside to make the exchange I walked back into the ranks without my horse, as I saw no reason why I should bother leading him along for my captors to ride, if he should ever get well. Fresh prisoners were added all the time, mostly cavalry and we marched along through the mountains the entire day. Stuart and his staff rode in our midst–rather an imprudent thing, I thought, for many of the men observed him closely with reference to a future meeting. I know it was in my mind every time I looked at him, though I had no malice and nothing to complain of regarding my treatment. Within a year he fell by the carbine of a cavalryman whose regiment who at this time was well represented among the prisoners.

"The day was a hard one for me, used to fatigue and fasting though I was. The roads were the roughest and the narrowest that could be found and I had eaten nothing since the previous day, having lost my haversack during the night. I was at last compelled to tell one of the guards that I was very hungry and he apologized for having nothing to give me, but, promised to see that I got something before we went much farther. He left the ranks soon and shortly afterward returned with some bread and butter which he divided with me. Later in the afternoon foragers brought us in rations collected from farm-houses.

"Just before sunset, as we were going through a gap, a rapid exchange of shots was heard ahead of us and both prisoners and captors became excited. A few moments later we were near enough to look out on the plain beyond; we saw the Confederates dismounting and deploying as skirmishers and my heart bounded as I saw my own regiment drawn up for a charge about five hundred yards away! I began to cry like a child; I thought I would be free again in about ten minutes, with my friends; that I would be armed and mounted as twenty-four hours before. The question, How did I know my own regiment! Naturally comes, and is easily answered. I could distinguish the companies by the color or their horses and knew the order of the squadrons in the line. The black horses of Troop C and the light bays of H formed the First Squadron, the sorrel horses of E and the dark bays of G formed the next and so on. The troops changed squadron often to suit the seniority of the captains and the squadrons changed positions in the regiment for the same reason, but the combination of companies before me now had been that of the regiment for a week at least.

"A call was made for sharpshooters and those who dismounted and presented themselves were supplied with cartridges and sent into the cornfield in front of us. But my regiment seemed disinclined to charge and merely threw out skirmishers to meet them. Some of the Confederates enthusiastically cried, "My! Won't the sharpshooters make it hot for that cavalry!"

"Though the firing became brisk, it wearied me; I wanted the charge because I was sure that a vigorous attack would send our guards fleeing without us in less than five minutes. One of them, a quiet, pleasant faced man, as were many of the others, noticed my dejected look, came to me and swinging himself from his saddle to a fence-rail took a Testament from his pocket and asked me if I objected to his reading a chapter aloud. I thankfully asked him to do so, as I had not had heart enough to read my own that day. He read a chapter in one of Paul's epistles and when he had concluded remarked that he would feel fifty percent better if the country were at peace and he were at home that night. I must add that while he was reading I held Quaker principles myself, for I was pained to think I was the enemy of that fair minded Christian young man who, like myself, thought he was right in engaging in a career of destruction to life and property. But we were both reminded that it was war and not peace by the call of, "More ammunition." For the sharpshooters and our guards had to supply it from their boxes, it being apparently scarce.

"Now is the time for the charge I thought. General Stuart had not more than three hundred men encumbered by as many prisoners and the regiment in front had five hundred in line. But while their commander hesitated, General Stuart whose genius and courage had gotten him out of many a difficulty proved himself equal to the present emergency. While his skirmishers were firing their last cartridges he made us fall in by fours and marched us two or three times across the opening. We were mistaken in the twilight for Confederate infantry coming up and then the whole column was moved along the edge of the corn-field, keeping the skirmishers between us and my regiment, which moved parallel with us, until darkness shut them out from view.

"The next morning Stuart's men were gone and we were guarded toward the Potomac by Pickett's division…"[15]

After passing through the little settlement of Pikesville, the staff members who had been on short rations for the past several days shortly found themselves dining at George Stephey's Tavern at the foot of the mountain near Red Run.

Stephey's Tavern, was a large brick dwelling, built in 1838 by Lewis Ripple (1779-1852) alongside the WGM turnpike in Pikesville, near the bridge crossing Red Run Creek. Lewis Ripple lived there until his death. He had been a sometime millwright,

---

15 *Battles and Leaders of the Civil War, Vol. III*, Edited by Johnson, R.V. & Bull, C.C., Century Publishers, New York, 1884 & 1888, p 429 ff.

wagoner, tavern keeper and postmaster along the turnpike at the summit of the South Mountain, the site of the "Battle of Monterey". He had moved to the mountain in the spring of 1811 (The enabling legislation for the Waynesburg, Greencastle and Mercersburg Turnpike was introduced in 1816.) from the Marsh district of Washington Township to open a wagon making and long distance hauling business near the place the headwaters of Red Run Creek crossed the turnpike at the site of the original Monterey Springs (now Rolando Woods Lions Club Park). This headquarters became known as "Zero" probably because it was the measured starting point for Ripple's wagons. In 1814, Ripple purchased Mooney's Tavern, which stood at the NW corner of the

Pen and Ink Sketch by Terry Mitchell, 1946

Stephey's Tavern

This house stood near the intersection of Old and new PA Rte. #16 at the foot of Rouzerville Hill. It was once host to General Robert E. Lee and his staff on their way back to Virginia. The small building was once a store. Lee spoke to his officers from the pump platform at the rear of the inn. (See over)

117

intersection of Monterey Lane and Charmian Road on the present Golf Course. It was a way station that became Ripple's Tavern. It was purchased from Patrick Mooney and in 1818, Ripple purchased additional lands known as "Bear Swamp" from Patrick's son, William. This land is now owned by Washington Township, Franklin County, PA and is preserved as a wetlands conservation district and has been proposed as an Interpretive Center for the Battle of Monterey Pass.

Lewis Ripple replaced Mooney's old wagon stand with a more substantial stone dwelling/tavern that became a popular store and layover for not only drovers and wagon drivers, but for the new stage lines traversing the pike and for the more well-to-do carriage trade. Ripple's Tavern was damaged by fire around 1820 and was immediately rebuilt. His Zero wagon business prospered and in 1837 Lewis Ripple was appointed postmaster of the new U.S. Post Office at Mt Zero. He served in this office until 1838, when he moved to Pikesville. The Zero Post Office was closed in April, 1839.

Ripples Tavern in Pikesville prospered as well as the one at Monterey and when Lewis Ripple died, in 1852, the title to the hostelry passed to George Stephey.

It is hard to imagine the prosperity along this turnpike, but we have a secondhand account of it from Miss Lottie Nevin who wrote "Mother (Matilda Ripple Nevin) told us many interesting stories of those long ago times...Travelers were coming and going all the time. Goods of all kinds were hauled from Pittsburg (sic) to Baltimore and from Baltimore to Pittsburg (sic), [With] immigrants from foreign lands in wagons and on foot, the wealthy people traveling by carriage and horseback, not a day [passed] without the excitement of arrivals and departures."[16]

Stephey's Tavern was a five bay, Georgian style common bond brick house with its front elevation featured two transom doors, which clearly distinguish it from the Federal style. The building is two stories high, ten rooms, with large chimneys and fireplaces at either end. The first floor was used as a tavern, hotel and store. It was once the home of Peter Rouzer, (1837-1915), the founder of

Photo from Author's Collection by Ryan D. Smith

Stephey's Tavern Pump

Stephey's Tavern pump platform at rear of inn where General Lee addressed his officers after dinner and where he presented George N. Stephey with the brass call bell (pictured) also is the kitchen at the center photo.

---

16 *Antietam Ancestors*, Vol. VII, No's 3 & 4, Winter 2000, p. 64, Waynesboro Historical Society, Waynesboro, PA 17268

Rouzerville. It was razed in 2007. The site then came into its present commercial use. The building's last private resident was Miss Mary K. Bonebrake who lived to be 107 years old.[17]

The old tavern enjoyed the reputation of playing host to General Robert E. Lee and General James Longstreet and their staff in the early afternoon on July 5, 1863 for dinner upon their withdrawal from the Battle of Gettysburg. Tradition has it that as the group of mounted men passed the tavern, one of the staff officers, probably Walter H. Taylor, General Lee's Adjutant and Aide-de-Camp, asked the owner and host, George N. Stephey, if he would serve them a meal. They were accompanied by a large number of foot soldiers.

Mr. Stephey had dinner prepared and served to the Generals and the staff officers. Daniel N. Stephey, then, but a boy of twelve was in the dining room and observed the men in gray very closely. "As was natural the big boots worn by General Lee attracted the youngster's attention. They reached above the officer's knees and were fastened there by straps.

"General Lee was a tall rather spare man, as he recalls him. He talked with his staff and after dinner went upon the pump bed at the rear of the house and made brief address to his men.

"When he offered to pay Mr. (George W.) Stephey for the meal and that gentleman refused to accept any remuneration, he (Lee) handed him the call bell, with the remark, "I'm going to let you

---

17 Pennsylvania Historic Resource Survey, PA. Historic and Museum Commission, Harrisburg, PA, Jan 1994. Marie Lanser Beck for Waynesboro (PA) Historical Society.

have this."[18]

"Mr. Stephey relates, incidentally, that the confederate soldiers were on their twenty acres of land on the western edge of Rouzerville for that day, they burned up all the fences and that the harvest, which was about ready to scythe, was all destroyed.[19]

Photos from Author's Collection

Stephey - Lee Artifacts

Shown at left is the brass Lee call bell (3 1/2 inches in diameter and 6 inches high). On the right is the folding camp stool left behind at the Stephey Tavern. The canvas seat is a replacement.

---

18 The call bell was probably incidental to Robert E. Lee. Who knows of a general officer, in any army, that carries on his person a handled call or school bell? It will be remembered that the wrecked wagon train was described as having strewn all types of plundered goods all over the roads during the retreat. General Lee probably picked up this artifact as he went along the way and would not have had it in his possession for very long. Stoner and others refer this gift to Stephey as a silver cup. There was also left behind, though not by Lee, a folding camp stool (as illustrated). These artifacts if they still exist, went west when Daniel Stephey and his wife Rosanna retired to live with one of their children.

19 Daily Record and Blue Ridge Zephyr, Waynesboro, PA. Tues, July 1, 1913, p.1.

CHAPTER SIX

Waynesboro, Lee's Livestock & Road To Hagerstown

As General Lee and his officers left Stephey's they headed west toward Waynesborough and crossed the bridge over Red Run and made their way along the Baltimore Pike, which was full of marching soldiers and wagon traffic, to the bridge over the east branch of the Little Antietam Creek, the bridge crossing the creek where Renfrew Museum is now located. Along their route they encountered several bivouac sites, the one close to Rouzerville, already mentioned, on the Mickley farm, east of town (where Eastland Hills is now developed), one at Green Hill Cemetery and at Gilberton (on the west side of the Hagerstown Road where Wayne Gardens now is)[1] at the top of this hill, they met the rear

---

1   Stoner, J. H., (1861-1946), <u>Historical Papers, Franklin County and the Cumberland Valley</u>, Compiled by Lucole Stoner, The Craft Press, Chambersburg, PA, 1947, p. 469.

guard Confederate pickets of the Mississippi Volunteers, together with a battery of Georgia Artillery. A little farther along they met the balance of the artillery and men of Brigadier General Carnot Posey's Mississippian Infantry lining the hilltop from the rear of the tollhouse, where Burns Hill Cemetery is now, eastward to the top of the hill at the rear of the present Waynesboro Hospital.[2]

"Just before entering Waynesboro a circumstance occurred that was both amusing and embarrassing. It seemed that when the Confederate army passed David Hoeflich's house where the hospital now stands, it was obliged to detour quite a distance through the fields on the opposite side of the road to avoid a hive of angry bees that were made so because several soldiers who had gone before had robbed them of their honey. All the men in Waynesboro could not have delayed the Confederate army a minute if they wanted to, nor compelled it to vary an inch in its course, but column after column of soldiers marched out through the field in order to avoid the angry little bees that held possession of that portion of our Monterey road…[3]

The confederates were taking no chances. They wanted no more disastrous rear guard routs like that had taken place the night before. The streets were lined with soldiers on their way to the Potomac River en route to their Virginia homeland. The easily recognized General was cheered and waved to as he passed along.

---

2   O.R. Series #2, Vol. 27, Part II, p. 676, Report of Col D. G. McIntosh to R.H.. Anderson, 3rd Army Corps CSA; See also D.G. McIntosh CSA, SHSP Vol. 37, 1909, p. 140 & Record Herald, Waynesboro, PA, Turs. 2 January, 1961, p.1.

3   Stoner, J.H. (1861-1946), Historical Papers, Franklin County and the Cumberland Valley. Compiled by Lucole Stoner, The Craft Press, Chambersburg, PA, 1947, p. 469

The party stopped briefly in front of 64 East Main Street. When they stopped their infantry guard rushed to the shade of the trees that lined Main Street. If they could find any type of tinder or small sticks, the soldiers would build tiny fires curb side and heat water in tins to brew coffee or chicory to drink. Dried chicory weed ground up was a popular substitute for coffee. The ladies of the town were kept continuously cooking and baking for this hoard (one housewife said she had baked over 100 loaves of bread). When he could, the Confederate soldier would beg hot water and perhaps a little brown sugar to make his brew.

Field hospitals were established in Waynesboro. Stoner said, "Two hospitals were improvised---one in the old Eastern Schoolhouse situated on Cottage Street---(at its intersection with Middle Street)---the other in the Western Schoolhouse where Doctor P.D. Hoover's house stands, (west of the Waynesboro Historical Society) in which both Confederate and Union soldiers lay side by side. Our women ministered to these men whether they wore the blue or the gray."[4]

Upwards of 20,000 to 30,000 troops, on the march, in wagons, on caissons and in bivouac, passed through Waynesboro from first light Sunday morning, July 5, 1863 until 9:00 a.m. on Tuesday, July 7, 1863. They bivouacked west of town where Frick Company is and on Funk's Hill just before you reach the Tick Ridge Road. They camped on both sides of the road where the Otterbein Center and Green Hill Cemetery are now located as well as in the woods at the Municipal Golf Course.

4   Ibid, p. 470

It took all of 2 days and a night for them to pass. The town was under Confederate control from Tuesday, June 23rd, 1863 until the U.S Army under the command of Brigadier General Thomas A. Neill, 3rd U.S. Cavalry and Light Artillery Division entered Waynesborough at about 3:00 p.m. on Tuesday, July 7th, 1863 and lowered the Stars and Bars that had flown over the Town Hall in Center Square. Remember that this was only part of the Confederate army; the other part was retreating by way of Leitersburg and Hagerstown to Williamsport. Lee had in total about 62,000 troops at Gettysburg and had lost killed, missing and wounded about 28,000. [5]

During this period there was only one dispatch sent from Waynesboro and that was on the last day of the occupation by the Union Army:

Headquarters, First Division

Department of the Susquehanna

Waynesborough, Pa. July 11,1863

"The Brigadier-general commanding calls the attention of the command to the certainty of an early engagement with the enemy and it is strictly enjoined upon brigade, regimental and company commanders to attend at once to the condition of arms and ammunition of the men under them. No time is to be lost in putting the arms in perfect order and seeing that the boxes are

---

5   Allan, Lt. Col. William, CSA, The Strategy of the Gettysburg Campaign, A Paper
     read before Military Historical Society of Massachusetts, May 9, 1887; Reprinted in
     the Gettysburg Papers, Vol. 1, p. 41.

filled with cartridges. The rations on hand must be cooked and put in haversacks, so that no detention will ensue when the order to march is given and also that the men may not suffer for food when it may be impossible for the supply trains to reach them.

By order of Brigadier General W.F. Smith. commanding First Division:

Alexander Farnham

Acting Assistant Adjutant General

Promulgated by order of Brigadier General Knipe:

Robert Munch

Acting Assistant Adjutant General

S/ Brig. Gen. Knipe[6]

All this passed without a shot being fired save one. Daniel Crouse, a Union soldier, home on furlough fired at a retreating Confederate marching in ranks from the second story window of 114 East Main Street. His aim was bad and the ball hit nothing. This saved the town from a reprisal that could have burned the town to the ground.

On Tuesday, July 7, when the advance guard of the Union Army sped into town in pursuit of the fleeing rebels, Samuel Clark in his enthusiasm ran out into the street in front of what was later the National Hotel to wave his hat to the troops. He remained a little too long and he was struck and knocked down by a horse. The entire cavalcade passed by without anyone stopping to help

---

6   O.R. Series 1, Vol. 27 (Part II), p. 264, General Knipe commanded the 125th NY Vols. And the 20th Connecticut Volunteers.

him. When all had gone, He jumped to his feet unhurt. Miraculously, all of the horses had stepped over him.[7]

Many a valuable was buried in the garden and vegetables or flowers planted over them on the slightest notice that the rebels were coming, but could not be left for long since the fear of them falling prey to local outlaws was great. The silver, jewels and cash would have to be dug up and reburied when the same old rumors of invasion burst forth. The irony of all this was that the plants seemed to thrive through all of the planting and replanting.

There was very little danger to the residents and the rebel soldiers were generally polite aside from boasting how they would win the war. Citizens were cautioned not to taunt or insult the soldiers and to put all intoxicating liquors out of reach.[8] The soldiers were authorized to take goods and provisions by force and to pay for them in Confederate scrip, which they printed as they needed it on a printing press they carried on a wagon. The scale of prices charged the army commissaries, presumably the average cost not the retail price. (Given in Confederate dollars) ...for bacon at $2.20 per pound, beef, 75 cents per pound on the hoof; lard $2.20 per pound; molasses, $6 per gallon; sugar $1.50 per pound. A coat cost $350; trousers $125; a hat $80 to $125 dollars; shirt $50; socks $10 per pair...The shrinkage in value of our (Confederate) currency continued with the progress of the war until, near the close, it almost ceased to have any purchasing

---

7 The Record Herald, Waynesboro, PA, Reminiscing, Weds. July 5, 1995, p. 5B
8 Bender, Lida Welsh, The Outlook, Civil War Memories, June 24, 1925,

power whatever.[9]

There was a great deal of skedaddling that went on. That is, people from other locales along the Mason-Dixon border were trying to move out of the reach of the invading southerners leaving their homes by carrying their goods and valuables and driving their livestock before them hastening North to avoid the real or imagined depredations and reprisals of the Confederates. Any rumor that the rebels were about to cross the Potomac from Virginia would bring hoards of refugees through the Waynesboro from out of town. Not that some Waynesbororians did not skedaddle too. Early on, the money and valuables were taken from the First National Bank by John Philips, the cashier, to Selinsgrove for safekeeping, where he stayed until after the Battle of Gettysburg.[10] Some of these fleeing migrants would pass through in the dead of night. Farmers would drive their horses and cattle ahead of them to the mountains and secluded places of refuge to save them from being commandeered. A week or so later, almost completely exhausted, they would drive them back home again finding the invasion rumor to have been false.[11]

There was some who doubted that Lee ever passed through Waynesboro, but the evidence that he stopped at the town pump in Center Square to water his horse and for an impromptu con-

---

9   Sorrel, G. Moxley (1838-1901), Recollections of a Confederate Staff Officer, W.S. Konecky Assoc. Inc., Smithmark Publishing, New York, 1994 (Previously published 1929)

10 The Record Herald, Waynesboro, PA, Rebels Occupy Waynesboro during Gettysburg Campaign, Friday, July 15, 1988

11 Bender, Lida Welsh, The Outlook, Civil War Memories; June 24, 1925

ference among his lieutenants, Hill, Longstreet, Ewell and Early.

These men and various members of their staff were crowded about the town pump when they were approached by a Mexican war veteran that had served under Lee in 1854. He was George W. Davis, a blacksmith in a coachworks, who lived close by at 11 South Church Street. He walked up to General Lee and put out his hand to greet his old commander, who was then standing on the platform of the pump. Evidently mistaking Mr. Davis

Photo from Author's Collection

Waynesboro Town Square

An 1882 view of the Town Pump and watering trough on the Diamond (Square) in Waynesborough (Waynesboro), PA. Here General Lee and his staff watered their horses. Lee met his old comrade-in-arms, George W. Davis from the Mexican War, who lived on South Church Street. The pump was moved to the SW corner of the public square in 1885.

intentions there was rattling of sabers among the officers and they instantly grouped themselves around General Lee for the purpose of resisting any attack on their chief. Then it was that General Lee recognized Mr. Davis and cordially shook hands with him and told him how happy he was to greet him as an old friend and as one of the soldiers under his command in the Mexican War. This incident certainly sets to rest any doubt about General Lee not passing through Waynesboro.[12]

Nor was the foregoing the only testimony to seeing Lee in the Center Square in Waynesboro. Dr. Miss Nevie C. Detrich whose office and home was in the building where the Candy Kitchen is, was in her medical offices with Mrs. John H. Johnston and they both saw the unmistakable Lee. [13]

In addition, Mrs. D.C. Weller, nee Mary C. Eckman, the daughter of the John C. Eckman, the manager of the Central Hotel on the Square, who was 14 years old at the time, saw him from the southwest second floor window of the hotel.[14]

Charles E. Besore who was then age 5 and lived on the NW corner opposite the Central Hotel remembered his mother with him at the window saying to him, "That gentleman with the beard is Robert E. Lee."[15]

---

12 Stoner, J.H. (1861-1946), Historical Papers, Franklin County and the Cumberland Valley. Compiled by Lucole Stoner, The Craft Press, Chambersburg, PA 1947, p. 466.

13 The Waynesboro Herald, Waynesboro, PA Gives Facts of General Lee's Stop Here to get Water at Old Town Pump article, July 5, 1929 and The Daily Record and Blue Ridge Zephyr, Article, Weds, July 2, 1913.

14 The Daily Record and Blue Ridge Zephyr, Waynesboro, PA, article, Thurs July 3, 1913, p. 1.

15 Record Herald, Waynesboro, PA Mountain Edition, July 5, 1929, p. 20

There was one contemporary news article albeit slightly derogatory from 1865:

SEEKING RELICS---We understand several Baltimore rebel sympathizers visited this place (Waynesboro) recently from Monterey and being told that General Lee, in 1863, watered his horse at the public pump on the Diamond, have been cutting chips from the water trough. Baltimore 'secesh' was this time misinformed. The stolen horse which bore the old traitor from an inglorious defeat, through our town, owing to 'pressing circumstances' was neither watered or fed."[16]

The junior officers surrounded their chief who stood on that pump as if they were a group of sons and he was their father. So great was their admiration for him! Everyone admired and loved General Lee, particularly the ladies who gravitated to him. Men held him as much an icon as our country's great leaders. In Richmond, there are but two monumental statues, those of George Washington and Robert E. Lee. Little children loved him and he loved them in return. He liked nothing more than to prattle with them, to tease them and to read and play games with them. There are those that knew him well that declared although he enjoyed a trick or practical joke to the utmost, he was never known to laugh. He would show his enjoyment of a joke by his quixotic half-smile but never a loud or raucous laugh. [17]

---

16 Village Record, Waynesboro, PA Friday, July 28, 1865, p.1
17 See Ranson, A.R.H., Harper's Monthly Magazine, February, 1911, Vol. CXII, No. DCCXXIX, p. 327

Make no mistake about it he was a military commander with a great deal of responsible experience and a fearsome one. His men feared and revered him. He seemed to be always thinking and to see everything and notice the actions of everyone, even to the lowliest recruit. He is said to have been able to wither you with a sentence, where military conduct was concerned and to make you feel "about this tall". He would make calm statements like "I see you have been avoiding our meetings lately" or "Your horses are wanting for lack of care. What will we do when we need them?" or "You have failed in your duty, I will not give you a second chance."[18]

There was a town rooster. A "long-legged, long-necked Shanghai that lived on the streets (and) who fearlessly threaded his way between their (marching feet of the rebels) and occasionally a man would take him up and carry him a few yards until a watchful officer ordered his release. That rooster paraded long after the last gun of the Confederacy was silenced."[19]

This is a reminder of the legend of General Lee's hen. "The acute food shortage in the winter camp pinched at headquarters and sometimes Lee's staff officers complained of the poor diet which Lee insisted on sharing with his soldiers. 'The Virginian loved good food, particularly fried chicken, barbecued shoat and roast beef (but) he ate only the simplest fare while in the field. While the General was the recipient of much fine food donated by residents near his camp or sent long distances by admirers, he was

---

18 Ibid, p. 328
19 Bender, Lida Welsh, <u>The Outlook</u>, Civil War Memories, June 24, 1925

quick to share it with his staff. Often he would distribute the surplus among his soldiers.'[20] The sparse rations were at least more temptingly served since Meredith, the negro, from the "White House", had been replaced by Bernard Lynch, an Irishman called "Bryan" who acted as (Lee's) mess steward. Among the presents showered on Lee (including a mattress) were chickens, too few in number for Lee to attempt to share with the others. Bryan killed these to serve when distinguished guests were present, such as Colonel Fremantle or Captain Schreibert of the Prussian Engineers.

Before it became the turn of the last hen to be roasted, she had developed the habit of going daily into the commanding general's tent and laying an egg under his cot. His staff officers were certain the hen showed him preference because of Lee's love of animals and fowl. The commanding general enjoyed an egg as his breakfast and the hen became a fixture at general headquarters."[21]

"Lee fond of domestic animals, appreciated her selection of his quarters and would leave the tent door (flap) open for her and wait elsewhere until her cackle informed him that he could return to his canvas home. She roosted and rode in his wagon, was an eyewitness to the Battle of Chancellorsville and there it is said she refused to lay until victory perched upon her general's plume, when she at once recommenced. Many month's she soldiered—participated, in her way, in the Battle of Gettysburg, but when the orders were given to fall back and the headquarters wagons had

20 Dowdey, Clifford Lee, <u>Lee, with Photos and with Maps by Bryant</u>, Little, Brown, Boston, 1965, p.333
21 Ibid. p. 334

been loaded, the hen could not be found. General Lee joined the others in a search for her and finally she was found perched on top of the wagon.

"In the fall of 1864, when Lee's headquarters were near Orange Court House, the hen had become fat and lazy and on one occasion when the general had a distinguished visitor to dine with him, Bryan, finding it difficult to procure suitable material, unknown to everyone, killed the hen. At dinner, the general was surprised to see so fine a fowl and all enjoyed it, not dreaming of the great sacrifice made upon the altar of hospitality."[22]

Lee's servants and staff were few. It was said that with Walter H. Taylor, his Asst. Adjutant General and Aide de Camp, who incidentally summered at Blue Ridge Summit in the years following the Civil War, Lee got along with a one-man head-quarters staff. (Walter Taylor's daughter, Bland and his grandson, Lee Taylor summered at Blue Ridge Summit well into the 1940's.) His manservant and it is believed, his wife Mary's father's ex-slave was Perry from Arlington who was with him throughout the war.[23] Lee it was said to have trouble rousting him from his bed on chilly mornings. Although he started the war with Perry as cook and mess attendant, Perry did not prove equal to the task. He then turned to Meredith, a freed slave from Rooney Lee's "White House Plantation", whose ability and serving habits did not suit Lee, while good enough for rough soldiers, his ability left something to

---

22 Lee, Fitzhugh, General Lee, D. Appleton Co.., New York, 1894, pp. 232-233
23 Perry was freed under the terms of the will of Geo. Washington Parke Custis, Lee's father-in-law, of which he was executor, on December 29, 1862, recorded in Huston Court, Richmond on Jan. 2, 1863

be desired when he had to entertain guests. Bernard Lynch, an Irishman, nicknamed "Bryan", finally filled the bill. In my opinion, "Bryan" was a household servant of Col. Joseph C. Ives, Chief Engineer on Lee's staff. Ives resigned his commission in the U.S. Army as did Lee and joined the Confederacy.

This might be a good place to put to rest a legend or myth naming Captain Joel Compton, CSA of Gretna, VA as Lee's wartime cook. The author has found several references to this in books over the years some attributed, some not. Upon research and investigation he has found nothing to substantiate this claim. One reference to this claim is given in the following letter:

"General Lee's wartime cook was Captain Joel Compton of Gretna, Virginia, a burly young man billed as the champion wrestler of the Army of Northern Virginia. A lively tradition among his descendants is that Joel inflicted the final casualty upon Grant's forces when he killed a bluecoat in a wrestling match following the surrender at Appomattox.

"Captain Compton lived until 1932, at ninety still defiantly Confederate.

"One of his great-grandsons was still "in uniform" as the war's centennial drew nigh: James I. (Bud) Robertson, Jr., PhD, editor of a scholarly journal published by the University of Iowa, Civil War History."[24]

---

24 Davis, Burke, The Civil War, Strange and Fascinating Facts, previously published as Our Incredible Civil War by Holt, Rinehart & Winston, Inc., NY, 1960. The 1982 edition distributed by Crown Publishers, Inc., New york

On page 5 Mr. Davis further acknowledges the assistance of James I. Robertson, Jr, editor of Civil War History for a story of his great-grandfather, General R.E. Lee's cook.

Research into this claim led the writer to the great-grandson of Compton, James I. Robertson, Jr, who was the adjunct Alumni Distinguished Professor of History at Virginia Polytechnic Institute and State University. He replied to my inquiry promptly,

> "I am afraid that information on my great-grandfather, John W. Compton has been grossly exaggerated. He was a member of the 57th Virginia Infantry Regiment. He was a member of Armistead's Brigade in Pickett's Charge at Gettysburg. However, he was never a Captain; an imsofar (sic) as being Gen'l. Lee's cook is concerned, that is a family legend and the kind of unverified story so present in descendants of Civil War soldiers. To my intense regret, no letters, diary or other writings exist about Pvt. Compton. I have his Bowie knife and canteen. Alas that is all.
>
> With best wishes,
>
> Sincerely,
>
> James I. Robertson, Jr.

The legend of Lee's milk cow is also an interesting little sidelight. "Notwithstanding the fact that our streets were crowded from curb to curb with marching soldiers, supply wagons, caissons, et cetera, there was seen by a few of our citizens, a soldier leading a solitary milk cow weaving his way through the throng. It seemed strange and out of place for this peaceful looking animal to be moving along with these accoutrements of war. It was learned, however, that this cow was General Lee's personal property and wherever the cow was to be seen it was taken for granted that its owner was not far away. It was called Lee's cow and it was said that he never used any milk except that supplied by his own cow. He is supposed to have exercised this care in order to protect himself against eating or drinking any food that might be adulterated.

Whether General Lee's cow came along with him from Virginia and went with him through the Battle of Gettysburg is not known. He may have changed cows frequently, for while his soldiers were in our valley they took thousands of cattle from our farmers and drove them toward the Potomac River. On account of the high water and because they could not wait until the waters reached a safe stage many of these cattle were carried down with the flood and drowned.

"It is a well known fact that considerable drinking was indulged in by the soldiers as well as the officers. It is related that one evening while a group of officers were assembled in (Lee's) tent, it was suggested (by Lee) as was perfectly natural, in those times, that they order drinks. The suggestion meeting with general approval each one was asked his preference. The question coming around to General Lee, he turned to his servant and said, "Bring me my favorite drink." Whereupon the servtitor soon appeared with an empty glass and a pitcher of milk and set it on the table. Not another word was said but the whole assembly felt at once that they were tactfully and politely administered a gentle rebuke by their commanding general. This incident lends color to the fact that General Lee drank milk and that he would likely want it fresh from his own cow"[25]

Jacob Stoner was obviously not aware of General Lee's liking for buttermilk and that he began each day with an egg. That he kept a cow was common knowledge among the headquarters company and whether he carried a churn to make buttermilk is not known, perhaps the motion of the wagon did the churning for him.

"Confederate veterans will smile reflecting recently and enviously on this story, says the News-Leader of Richmond. Think of the affluence of an army the commander of which carried two milch cows with him wherever he went. The editor proceeds to call up from the past a personal and picturesque bit of American history:

"The old gray coats that grow hungry even now in reflecting upon the privations of the later years of the war between the States, the thing seems inconceivable! Why the mess of General Lee never boasted a single cow, except for a very brief period. Its solitary hen, the pride of Cook Bryan's heart, was guarded with jealous apprehension, because no man knew when the hunger of some passing soldier might not deprive General Lee of his daily egg, the chief staple of his diet. In fact, there was a suspicious element of mystery about the final disappearance of that hen. All the winter she nested in a headquarters wagon alarmed neither by

---

25 Stoner, J.H., <u>Historical Papers of Franklin County and the Cumberland Valley, Pennsylvania</u>, compiled by his wife, Lucole Stoner, The Craft Press, Chambersburg, PA 1947, p. 473

the roar of the cannon nor the clatter of the soldiers horses. She was as regular in depositing her egg for her beloved commander as Stuart's cavalry was in its scouting. But when the army began to move for the final summer campaign the hen whose cackling had been constant music at headquarters and whose unabashed presence had graced many a council of war was nowhere to be found. In his charity to all men, Lee explained that the hen must have strayed away; but deep in his heart, Bryan had a conviction that it was not a casual stray, but of stealing. Some irreverent soldier, Bryan maintained secretly slew and ate the sacred fowl, whose egg had helped in making the battle-plans of the Army of Northern Virginia.

"And to think of the gallons of fresh milk---gallons in the private mess of Marshall Haig, whether the commander was pressing his offensive or hurrying to an endangered front! The old Confederates never had fresh milk and when they had buttermilk, the fact that it was kept in a jug usually raised false hopes that the shattering of which left no stomach for butter. Was it not so that famous day when Lee invited his staff and a few visiting generals to have a drink? There had been a report detailed and precise of a certain bottle of very old apple brandy which some admirer had prest (sic)upon General Lee. The commander, of course, had not touched it, but men whispered excitedly that he always carried it with his headquarters baggage. When, therefore, he smilingly invited his guest to have a drink, instantly came visions of that bottle uncovered in great good humor and passed from parching lip to cracking throat. But, the corpus delecti proved to be a jug, not a bottle and what was a much more serious matter, despite an insinuating gurgle when at last it poured forth its contents, they proved to be buttermilk, not brandy. Lee, history reports in all solemnity was the only man that enjoyed either the joke or the dram!"26

The commanding general and staff wound their way west along Main Street and made at left turn onto Leitersburg Street (now Potomac Street) and followed the Confederate crowd out of town toward Hagerstown crossing the twin covered bridges across the Little Antietam (which they burned behind them, after all had crossed. The stream being in flood stage, was too high and roiling to safely ford.)

---

26 Editor, <u>The Literary Digest Magazine</u>, August 16, 1919, p.56

CHAPTER SEVEN

A Bridge To Build and A River To Cross

Lee and his lieutenants made up the vanguard of Longstreet's corps as they left Waynesboro, and headed across the twin-covered bridge spanning swollen confluence of East and West Branches of the Little Antietam Creek, not long before it was burned by the rear guard of the Confederate Ewell's troops mid-afternoon on that Sunday the 5th of July, 1863. The ford near the bridge was barely passable across the two branches. The approaches to it had been cut to pieces by the passing ordnance and wagon wheels. Lee labored the ten miles to Leitersburg slowly among the with-drawing Confederate troops estimated at 20,000 soldiers.[1]

---

1   Manuscript note from author's collection. Paper of Henry and D. Snively Smith, Waynesboro, Franklin Co. Pa., contemporary merchants and restauranteurs. This is an eyewitness report.

Brig. General Thomas H. Neill Commander of the 3rd Brigade, 2nd Division of the Sixth Infantry Corps, USA and McIntosh's Brigade of cavalry and with two pieces of light artillery (10 pound Parrott guns) said that he, "pursued the enemy rapidly at a trot to Waynesborough, leaving his infantry behind and upon arriving there found the rear guard of the Confederates had left for Hagerstown about three hours before (that was about noon on July 7th)" Neill said, "He pushed through the town and took the Hagerstown Pike and about two miles out found that the enemy had burned the bridge over the Antietam at that point." He said, "This prevented him from crossing his artillery." His cavalry pushed forward to about four miles from Hagerstown and found the enemy strongly posted at all the fords and bridges on the Antietam amply covering the rear of Ewell's Corps.[2]

The Confederates, upon arriving at Hagerstown, moved south of the town to the Lappans Road, somewhere between St. James and the Williamsport crossing. Ewell's Corps constituted the rear guard and continued only as far as the intersection of the Hagerstown Pike and the Long Meadow Road, south of

---

Footnote #1 (Cont'd)

"Rebels entered Waynesboro, Thurs June 18th, 1863, Friday 19th, 90 took dinner on Saturday the 20th;

About 1500 to 2000 left Sunday afternoon; [on] Monday 22nd between 5000 to 8000 thousand left; Tuesday 23rd & 24th Scouts & Stragglers; Friday 26th Gen'l. A.P. Hill came to town- left Saturday morning 27th, supposed 20,000; 3rd July big Battle at Gettysburg; 5th; Sunday morning train captured; Sunday evening Battle at Unger's Gap; 6th Monday 1 o'clock (a.m.) rebels retreating through Waynesboro till Tuesday at 9 o'clock (a.m.) & our calvalry (sic) came in to town at 3 o'clock P.M."

2   O.R. Series 1, Vol. 51, (Pt. 1) p. 196. Report of Brig Gen Thomas H. Neill commanding Light Division of Army of the Potomac. See also: O.R. Vol. 27 Series 2, (Pt. 1) . pp. 678-680

Leitersburg where they picketed the roads and bridges against an advance on their rear, turned westward and headed for Paramount and came to the intersection of the Hagerstown-Chambersburg Road, which we now know as the Marsh Pike.[3]

This was about one mile north of Hagerstown. The army bivouacked in the fields along the Leitersburg and Marsh Pikes and as the sun set they pitched their headquarters tents in the fields adjoining Long Meadow Church of the Brethren and used the church building as their office. The Confederate bivouac centered on Paramount (Paradise) Hill at the intersection of Longmeadow Road and the Marsh Pike.

This old church has a curious origin and an interesting history aside from serving as a Confederate headquarters for nearly a week in the summer of 1863. The Longmeadow Brethren date their beginnings to the time of Thomas Cresap's land grant in the mid-1700's and the congregation takes its name from the name of his land patent. The church had no formal organization for nearly one hundred years after it began holding its first services in the homes of the members and later at the Antietam Forge settlement, which we now call Rock Forge.

"Thomas Cresap enlarged his holdings of land twice. The original grant was made in 1739 by Lord Baltimore and was for 300 acres in (then) Frederick County, as the westernmost counties of Maryland were known (i.e.) Washington, Allegany and Garrett Counties. Cresap built a stone structure which served as a fort

---

3   O.R. Series 1, Vol. 27 (Pt. II) p. 472; Early, Maj. Gen. Jubal A. Report, 22 August. 1863.

and a dwelling place. The original dwelling is still standing as a National Register Historic Landmark...very little remains of the fort. Part of the foundation was utilized as the foundation for a later addition to the house. Cresap was the earliest settler in those parts. Cresap called his original grant "The Long Meadows". He had previously settled on a grant from Lord Baltimore, who had made a number of grants to Catholics well north into Penn's territory. It was an attempt by the Carrolls to advance the boundary of their land as far to the north as they could. His incursions were hotly contested by the Penns for many years.

Cresap had first settled and built a fort against Indian sieges as far north along the west bank of the Susquehanna opposite present day Columbia, PA. In this enterprise, encouraged by the Carrolls, he was ill received by Penn's German immigrants, who in a fit of mob violence, set his fort afire and in the fracas one man was killed, Cresap and four of his cohorts were captured and imprisoned in Philadelphia for a year around 1736. Upon his release he obtained a grant for "The Long Meadows" north of Hagerstown. This was the earliest land grant in Maryland, west of the Blue Ridge.[4]

---

4   Henry, J. Maurice, History of the Church of the Brethren in Maryland, Brethren
     Publishing House, Elgin, Illinois, 1936 p185 See also: Longmeadow
     Remembered, Monograph or Brochure?. Published by the Longmeadow Lions
     Club, Hagerstown, MD 21742-2678, 1987. p. 2;
     Note: There has long been some confusion in the names of Paradise and
     Paramount. The truth is; these names describe the exact same location at the inter-
     section of Longmeadow Road and the Marsh Pike. There has been a school at the
     intersection of the Marsh Pike and Longmeadow Road for many years and it was
     early called Paradise School and little community around it Paradise. The original
     25' square stone one-room school was razed in 1853 and a brick school replaced
     it. In 1915, a new two-room was built. In June, 1901, when Paradise needed a

146

"The membership (of the Longmeadow Church of the Brethren) centered on Paramount (Paradise) Hill where a school was built in 1832 and was used for both a school and preaching services until 1850.

"The building fell into neglect and a meeting was called in 1853 to meet on the site in an attempt to raise enough money to remodel the (school) house. Captain Henry Clapper presided as chairman. George Petre doubled his first subscription but his effort failed and the house was abandoned.

"Jonas Rowland was present at the meeting and argued that a new brick church should be built (and used as a school) instead of spending money on the old house. Some sharp differences of opinion developed and Rowland offered to show his good faith when he agreed to burn the brick and erect the church at his own expense. (This he did.) The first building was 40 by 30 feet and it was finished and dedicated in 1853...

The membership grew and a new church addition was planned... The new place of worship was 40 by 70 feet. It was dedicated in 1881."5

This building has long since had several additions, but it stands on the original 2 - acres donated by Jonas and Ann Gilbert

---

post office it was discovered that there was already an existing Paradise P.O. in Baltimore Co. near Catonsville. So Paradise became Paramount. A later school building, one built in 1915 was heavily damaged by a fire caused by lightning on May 18, 1950 and was then completely rebuilt.

Same source: (Ibid?) Longmeadow Remembered, p. 15. See also: Baltimore Sun, Mon., 1 August 1898, p. 56

Further Note: For more see: The History of the Cresaps, Compiled by Jos. Ord Cresap and Bernarr Cresap. Pub by The Cresap Society, McComb, MS, 1937.

5   Ibid, pp. 186-7.

Rowland for the first house of worship. Their farmland adjoined the original Cresap Long Meadows land grant.

Ann Gilbert Rowland, the wife of Jonas Rowland, was a singular and courageous woman, the daughter of the pioneer, Jacob Gilbert. She was born on December 9, 1811. "She was vigorous in speech, commanding in personality and convincing in argument. She matched herself against both men and women in her crusading spirit of reform. She was feared by liquor dealers and weak politicians but revered by all classes.

"When Jacksonian democracy was sweeping away the strong and powerful and extending the franchise to the common people, Ann was on the front line urging reform; when Elder Daniel Reichard started his campaign against the use of liquor...Ann Rowland entered the fight with the crusading spirit of a Carrie Nation.

Photo from History of the Church of the Brethren in MD

Longmeadow Church of the Brethren

"When Captain Henry Clapper called the meeting at Paradise [sic] (Paramount) School in 1853 to raise enough money to remodel the school building, Ann Rowland sent her opponents down to defeat and donated two and one-half acres of land for a new church. She and her husband, Jonas, burned the brick, laid the foundation and built the church at their own expense. (As had been promised) Ann was not easily daunted or turned back. She was born to dare and do good things."

"General Robert E. Lee pitched camp for nearly a week at Longmeadow in 1863 and notified the people in the community that his headquarters would be in the Dunker church. Ann Rowland was the first visitor General Lee had when she called on him to hand over the Bible on the pulpit to her. The general arose from his improvised desk where he was engaged in writing and stood for a few moments in silence. A rare personality was standing in his presence. With great admiration and courtesy, General Lee said, "Mrs. Rowland, we use this Bible in our morning worship. If it is left here, General Robert E. Lee pledges his honor that this Holy Word shall be kept safely and no harm will come to this place of worship."[6]

---

6   Ibid, p. 301 ff; Note: There has long been a controversy over whether Mrs. Rowland actually confronted an officer, *other* than the unmistakable Lee, who pledged Lee's word of honor to give his own subordinate rank more prestige. There has also long been a discussion about whether the Church was used as Lee's Headquarters during the invasion on his way north *to* Chambersburg instead of during the retreat prior to the Battle of Gettysburg rather than during the withdrawal from the battle. The Rebels were traveling too fast on their way North, during the invasion to have stayed a week. In any case, the legend persists that it was indeed General Lee that Ann Rowland had confronted.

Many soldiers came to the home of Ann Rowland to buy meat. She suspected that they wanted to find where her provisions were kept and when they came, she made them wait at the front gate. One day the soldiers started to follow her but she turned with a butcher knife in her hand and said, 'Don't you dare make another step.' The men obeyed and remained in their tracks until she returned with the meat."[7]

Ann Rowland's second encounter with General Lee was over another matter of honor. "All the Rowland horses excepting one were taken. Old Jen the favorite and indispensable driving horse being the exception. Jen was hidden in the storage cave under the approach to the large barn and posts were placed around the door to distract attention. However, they did not count on her (Old Jen) becoming lonely and attempting to attract attention by her neighs. As a result of them, she was discovered by the soldiers and taken from her place of concealment. Ann Rowland immediately made her way to General Lee, who was encamped at Longmeadow and asked for the return of her driving mare. He replied, 'If you are so brave as to request the return of your horse, you shall have her back.' Old Jen was returned but was later taken again...

"Soldiers were encamped everywhere...Mrs. Rowland baked some bread for them in addition to selling them meat. The meat had been hidden above the fireplace in an outbuilding called the smokehouse. This place of concealment could be reached only by climbing a ladder and none but the immediate family knew of it.

---

7   Ankrum, Freeman, Sidelights on Brethren History, The Brethren Press, Elgin, Illinois, 1962. p. 126.

"During these trying days General Lee placed a guard at the Rowland barn to prevent destruction and stealing. The guard was a Methodist preacher; he told members of the Rowland family that even though he was in the army he had never shot anyone."[8]

At the time of the Civil War, Mrs. Rowland was a widow, her husband, Jonas, having died in 1855, soon after the first Longmeadow Church was built. He left her with eight of their ten children (living) upon his passing.

"Ann Rowland possessed a keen and sane judgment on financial matters. She came from a wealthy family and had inherited five hundred acres of land. She managed economically and gave liberally. Her home was a model of simplicity and righteous living. None were too poor to find welcome at her table."[9]

She passed away on September 28, 1888. There was an unexplained attempt to rob her grave on the eve of her burial. The culprits were never caught and their motive was never explained. Her body was imme-diately transferred on September 30th to the cemetery in Hagerstown.

The Brethren Press

**Ann Rowland
(1811-1888)**

---

8 Ibid., pp. 125-126.
9 Henry, J. Maurice, <u>History of the Church of the Brethern</u>.

Later, when the new cemetery was laid out at the Longmeadow Church, Jonas Rowland and his beloved wife, Ann were interred there.

General Lee was uneasy when he headquartered at the Longmeadow Brethren Church, he was deeply concerned that his troops would be trapped against the swollen Potomac River although his the men made a desperate effort to ferry the wounded from the wagon train in rowboats the going was slow and there were few conveyances to transport those who weren't able to walk. Lee and his entire Army were trapped by a river to cross. He had every right to be fidgety. He hadn't been well since the Battle of Chancellorsville where on the 30th of March, 1863, his "illness began as a cold accompanied by a sore throat and chest pain. Lee had also suffered from severe pain in his left arm which he had concealed from every one but his wife. It is a shame there is no written diagnosis of this by his attending physicians, first tended by Dr. Lafayette Guild, the Confederate medical chief and later by Dr. S.M Bemiss. It is assumed that he was suffering from acute pericarditis (an inflammation of the heart)."[10] He had suffered a mild heart attack with none of the after effects that made it apparent. These maladies, shortness of breath and chest pain, Lee suffered from the short time of his confinement after the Battle of Chancellorsville until the time of his death.

---

10   Mainwaring, Richard D. M.D. & Tribble, Curtis G., M.D. The Cardiac Illness of General Robert E. Lee, The Surgeon's Library, Dep't. of Surgery University of Virginia Health Sciences Center, Charlottesville, VA. SURGERY JOURNAL, Volume 174, March 1992, p. 237 ff.

On April 5, 1863, just before Chancellorsville while he was confined to bed at Thomas Yerby's house near Mine Gap Road and Hamilton Crossing south of Fredericksburg from here on the battlefield he wrote his wife, Mary: "I am suffering with a bad cold... and was threatened, the doctors thought, with some, malady which must be dreadful, if it resembles its name, but which I have forgotten. ... I have not been so very sick, though I have suffered a good deal of pain in my chest, back and arms. It came in paroxysms, was quite sharp. . . but they have passed off. . . . and I am enjoying the sensation of a complete saturation of my system with quinine." From Fredericksburg, VA. S/ R.E. Lee[11]

While his army was restricted at Williamsport, he was constantly on the move inspecting his lines of defense, directing improvements to the works, ever on the lookout for a Union advance that would threaten his compromised army. He and Early spent less than a week, more like four days, at Paramount and much of this time General Lee was somewhere else, perhaps at Broadfording or Williamsport or Huyetts or St. James supervising the placement of artillery and the digging of entrenchments.

Longmeadow was part of a group of headquarters from which Lee could "Granny" over his lines. Where he could assess and survey the places along his lines of defense while all the while anticipating an attack on his cornered forces crowded along the banks of the flooded Potomac. As the flood waters slowly receded Early's division was subsequently moved, on the 10th of July from

---

11 Dowdey and Manarin, Edit., The Wartime Papers of R. E. Lee, pp.427-429, New York, Bramhall House, 1961.

Longmeadow to a position in support of Hill's troops along the National Road (Route 40) southwest of Hagerstown.[12]

General Lee moved his headquarters to a spot along Hagerstown-Williamsport Pike. It was in a park-like setting but he wasn't there long, the level of the river was at long last receding. "He pitched his tent under a large elm tree which stood on the south side of the Hagerstown Pike, in the "cool hollow" northeast of "Mt. Tammany" and "Van Lear".[13]

Photo from Maryland Historic Trust - 1967

Mt. Tammany Manor

Tammany, as it is locally called, is a historic manor house of the Van Lear's, built around 1780 and is now located in the heart of a highly developed area just north of Old Route 11, between Williamsport and Halfway, near the interchange of Interstate 70 and 81. Lee pitched his tent just across the road from the entrance of today's Tammany Lane.

---

12 OR, Series 1, Vol 2, Pt. II, Excerpt Report of Gen Jubal A. Early. 22 Aug. 1863, p. 472.

13 Wolfe, George "Hooper", Program & Brochure, Civil War Centennial; Published by Mayor and Council, Williamsport, MD, 1962.

"Mt. Tammany" or just "Tammany" as it was locally called was situated northeast of Williamsport, just north of Route 11, and was the country mansion of the town, along with "Van Lear", another mansion house. Both of the houses were built on a south facing area of level ground along the Williamsport Pike and were built by the well-to-do Van Lear's. Mt. Tammany is believed to have been built in the 1780's by Matthew Van Lear, a wealthy canal commodity trader and banker. It remained in possession of Van Lear descendants until 1928 and is a National Historic Register Landmark, it is situated on a 2.6 acre plot of land, now surrounded by dense residential development. The Van Lear family was related by marriage to William Findlay (Born in Mercersburg, PA) in 1768 and died in Harrisburg, PA in 1846. He served as Governor of Pennsylvania from 1817 to 1820). The family was also intermarried with the family of William Henry Harrison, 9th president of the United States from Ohio.[14]

From Tammany, Lee was in close proximity to the construction of the pontoon bridge crossing of the Potomac at Falling Waters, where he could lend personal advice to his many subordinates and to supervise the deployment of the Confederate Army all along the line of defense for his troops from St. James to Huyetts Crossroad. Being the engineer that he was, General Lee paid particular attention to the orientation and direction of the dug entrenchments all along his lines of defense.

---

14 Maryland Historical Trust Survey 4004, 1967, Uia-I-023; District 26, Map 48, Parcel 329.

"Gen. Lee rode into Williamsport in the evening and sat on a large sandstone mounting stone at the corner in front of the old Taylor Hotel (the NW corner of Potomac and Conochocheague Streets) while he conversed with Mr. Taylor and some of the local citizens."[15]

General Lee was a little worse for the wear since the battle at Gettysburg. In the days following the battle, on July 4th and 5th, he

Taylor Hotel 2008

Photo of the Old Taylor Hotel, now a Quick Stop at the corner of Conochocheague and Potomac streets in Williamsport the location of the sandstone mounting block that General Lee would sit on in an evening and talk with the idlers and loafers in front of the hotel. The mounting block has recently disappeared, fallen victim of a sidewalk and storm drainage public works project.

---

15 Wolfe, George "Hooper," Program & Brochure; Civil War Centennial; Published by Mayor and Council, Williamsport, MD. 1962

had faced daunting decisions as to how to stage the most dangerous withdrawal that a commanding officer ever had to face up to that time. He had had no rest or sleep for at least forty hours after Gettysburg and he had been stricken with a devastating bout of diarrhea. This attack was probably initiated by the stress and excitement of the battle and the realization of the certainty of defeat on last day of the battle after Pickett's Charge and his Army's tremendous loss of men in the direct frontal attack on Cemetery Hill.

General Lee, while at Williamsport, was fidgety. He rode his lines tirelessly supervising the construction of earthworks and the sweep of his artillery batteries. After all, Lee was no stranger in engineering fortifications. From the time of his graduation from the US Military Academy, his work had been primarily supervising the building or modernizing forts. He oversaw the work of his engineers and pioneer companies in the rebuilding of the pontoon bridge across the swollen river at Falling Waters. These constructors had salvaged lumber from the flood debris, the output of, at least, two local sawmills along with lumber salvaged from the warehouses (Cushwa's) near the Williamsport turning basin.

Lee weighed the tenuous position of his Army, all the while waiting for the attack of Meade's forces that he knew was superior in number and armament to his own.

Lee's legion may have been exhausted but they were used to hardship, they were ready to fight to the last man, of the twenty odd thousand shoeless soldiers, 4000 to 5000 wagons and ambulances with a river to cross.

Finally the bridge was finished. The last pontoons and decking were in place and the crossing begun on July 13, 1863. General Lee mounted his horse, crossed the bridge and watched the crossing from an elevated muddy bank on the Falling Waters side. Almost all of the livestock, some 5 thousand head of cattle, horses, mules, swine and sheep had to be driven across, when the swollen river had fallen enough.

Sometime during that night Lee asked Longstreet to take over the supervision of the crossing so he could get some rest. Considering the circumstance of the driving rain off and on all night, the crossing went well despite the roads being knee-deep in mud and a few wagon breakdowns and accidents.[16]

On the morning of the 14th of July, it happened. "There, said General Lee. "I was expecting it, the beginning of the attack."[17] They came on fast and surprised the Confederates who had no pickets out. It was Kilpatrick with his 6th Michigan Cavalry who had caught them unaware, scattering them to the four winds. It was almost a complete rout, but somehow the Rebs regained their arms did an about face and fired volley after volley into the Union Cavalry ranks. Those that were unarmed or were of out of ammunition fought it out with clubbed muskets and fence rails and axes. The bridge crossing defenses closed up, the cavalry was driven back, but, not before General Pettigrew was mortally

---

16 Longstreet, James; <u>From Manassas to Appomattox, Memoirs of the Civil War in America</u>, J. B. Lippincott, Co. Philadelphia, 1869.
17 Sorrel, G. Moxley, <u>Recollections of a Confederate Staff Officer</u>, Wiley, Edit. McCowat-Mercer Press, Jackson, Tenn., 1958.

wounded. The Confederate withdrawal continued as the Union Cavalry waited for reinforcements. Meade had missed his chance.

The damp, disheveled, shoeless rebel columns moved on in their own improvident way toward Martinsburg, a town that had every available building with any space at all crowded with Confederate wounded, that had arrived there nearly a week ahead of them. Their General was much relieved that they had made their escape from the Yankees at last. His poorly provisioned, poorly clothed and poorly armed troops would live to fight another day; would live to fight another two years, as a matter of fact. They passed through Martinsburg and moved on to the same bivouac they had used on their way north at the little village of Bunker Hill. Heavily picketed and safe at last.[18]

---

18 Dowdey, Clifford Lee & Lewis H, Manarin, <u>The Wartime Papers of Robert E. Lee</u>; DaCapo Press, A subsidiary Plenum Pub. Corp. NY, 10013, 1961 & Unabridged Publications of Boston, 1961 p.551 Letter #522. See also OR Series I, Vol. 27, Pt 1, pp. 302 & 310.

Traveller Appendix
(Continued from Footnote 4, Page 8)

General Lee had many mounts during his career, namely: Grace Darling, Richmond, Brown Roan, Ajax and Lucy Long. Richmond had been presented to Lee by some of his admirers in 1861, soon after he joined the Confederate cause. This stallion died soon after the Battle of Malvern Hill (1 July 1862)

Brown Roan went blind early in the war and was given to a farmer. Ajax, Lucy Long and Traveller accompanied Lee to Lexington after the war. Ajax impaled himself on a gate latch and died prior to Lee's own demise in 1870. Traveller died of lockjaw in June 1871, soon after the General's death. His bones were on display at the Washington and Lee Museum from 1907 until 1962 when they were buried at Lexington, Virginia. Lucy Long lived on until 1891. (See Lee's Dispatches 1862-1865, pp. 4 & 5: Jefferson Davis, Notes and References on Robert E. Lee)

Traveller was the General's particular favorite and a privileged character at the Lee home in Lexington where he was allowed to remain in the front yard, where the grass was greenest and freshest, notwithstanding the damage he would do to the flowers and shrubbery. Lee took great pleasure in watching Traveller enjoy himself, often watching from a window while the horse grazed. He would allow no corn to be fed to him, saying he had plenty of that kind of fare during the war. The General seemed to be more demonstrative toward his old companion in battle than we seem to find in his nature toward men. He was often seen to enter the front gate, leave the walk, approach the old horse and caress him for a minute or two before entering the front door, as though they both bore a common grief in their memory of the past." (Confederate Veteran, Vol. 1. p. 265; Lee, Jr Recollections, p. 167)

When Traveller was brought up to the door, Lee would walk all around him, looking carefully at the horse, saddle, bridle, bit and shoes. If the blanket was not arranged to suit him, the General would hold the bridle while the saddle was removed, then he would take off the blanket himself, spread it out, smooth it and fold it to suit his idea of fitness and replace it on Traveller's back. He would then carefully superintend the putting on and girthing of the saddle. Traveller appreciated this love and sympathy and returned it as much as was in a horse's nature.

One afternoon, the General accompanied his daughter and a friend to a ferry landing, he riding in the saddle, they in a buggy. In saying their goodbyes, Lee dismounted and hitched Traveller to a post and stepped aboard the ferry.

Shortly, someone called out that the horse was loose. Sure enough, the gallant gray was on his way up the road, increasing his speed as a number of men and boys tried, in vain, to stop him. (The horse was probably thinking the General had no need more need for him when he stepped on the ferry.) The General called to the crowd to stand still and gave a peculiar low whistle. Traveller stopped, pricked up his ears. The General gave the whistle the second time and the horse, with a glad whinny, turned and trotted back to his master, who patted and praised him, before tying him again.

In answer to the astonishment of the bystanders at the creature's docility, General Lee observed that he did not see how any man could ride a horse for any length of time with out a perfect understanding being established between them. (Lee, Jr Recollections: p. 265)

Lee and Traveller were totally bonded to each other. It was astride Traveller that Lee had his narrowest wartime escape. During the heat of battle, it was in Lee's nature to become exorcised and caught up in the conflict. It was his intuition to lead. Particularly, when the need for action was immediate, he placed himself forward into the thick of it. At the Battle of the Wilderness, the soldiers seized Traveller's bridle and the General was forced back with the cry of "Lee to the rear!" There was no one steed more recognizable to the men than Traveller, or any other officer more visible. After this first instance, when the battle had spread, the General again recklessly exposed himself to open fire attempting to conduct his command. Again came the cries,

"Go back! General, go back!" During this second episode, he came under such heavy artillery fire that Traveller reared uncontrollably. While being calmed, he reared up a second time and as he did so, a solid shot passed just under his girth. Had he not lunged at that instant, Robert E. Lee and his beloved mount would have both been killed. (<u>Freeman</u>, Vol. III, p. 237; <u>Southern Historical Society Papers</u>, Vol. 8, p. 107; see also <u>SHSP</u>, Vol. 14, p.525)

Lee first saw this horse in the fall of 1861 and it was apparently love at first sight, at least, this was so on General Lee's behalf. He took a great fancy to the steed and called him "my colt". Traveller was four years old at this time. He had been bred and broken, by a Mr. Johnston, near the Blue Sulphur Spring in western Virginia. He was of Gray Eagle stock and had taken first prize in his age class at the County Fair for the years 1859 and 1860, under the name of Jeff Davis. (General Ulysses S. Grant also had a horse named Jeff Davis.) When Lee first saw him, Major L. Broun, who had bought him from Captain James W. Johnston, owned him. Johnston was the son of the man that bred him.

General Lee saw "his colt" once again in South Carolina ridden by Major Broun's brother and again admired him. He was offered to the General as a gift, which he declined. (It was characteristic of Robert E. Lee to never accept a gift or favor in which he could not promptly reciprocate.) Lee did offer to buy the horse if he would be allowed to take him on a trial basis. Major Broun then wrote to his brother and Traveller was sold to the General for $200 in Confederate currency in February 1862. Thomas L Broun had paid $175 in gold for him in September of 1861. There was some question about the horse's name. His registered name was most certainly Jeff Davis, however, in several instances, and he was called Greenbrier, perhaps meaning the prizewinning horse from Greenbrier County. In the construction of the interior Confederate defense lines between Charleston and Savannah, Lee covered 115 miles, most of it by train, but for 35 miles of the journey he rode the beautiful horse called Greenbrier. Because Greenbrier showed such great endurance and strength...General Lee thought him a fine traveler. Lee renamed him Traveller and the horse soon became part of the legend that was Lee. (Lee, Fitzhugh, General Lee, p. 299; Freeman, Robert E. Lee, Vol. I, p. 609; Confederate Veteran, Vol. I, p. 292)

Bibliography

Agassiz, George R. Editor, *Meade's Headquarters 1863-1865*, Atlantic Monthly Press, Boston, 1922

Alexander, Edward Porter, *Fighting for the Confederacy*, Personal Recollections, Gary Gallagher, Ed. Chapel Hill; University of North Carolina Press, 1989

Alexander, Edward Porter, *Military Memoirs of the Confederacy* New York, Scribners, 1907

Allan, William, Lt. Col. CSA, *The Strategy of the Gettysburg Campaign*, A paper read before the Military Historical Society of Massachusetts.

Ambrose, Stephen E. *Crazy Horse and Custer*, Doubleday, New York, 1976

Ankrum, Freeman, *Sidelights of Brethren History*, The Brethren Press, Elgin, Illinois, 1962

Bachelder, John B. *John Bachelder's History of the Battle of Gettysburg* Ladd and Ladd, Editors, Dayton OH. Morningside Press 1997

Bibliography (Cont'd)

Bandy & Freeland, Compilers, 2 Vols, *Gettysburg Papers*, Morningside Bookshop Press, Dayton, Ohio, 1978

Barber, James G. Editor, *Faces of Discord*, Harper, Collins Pub. Smithsonian, Washington, DC, 2006

Barnett, Louise K., *Touched by Fire*, Henry Holt, New York, 1996

Bates, Samuel, P and Richard, J.F., *History of Franklin County*, PA., Chicago, Warner & Beers, 1887

Beale, R.T.L.*History of the 9th Virginia Cavalry in the War Between the States*, Richmond, Va; Johnson Publishing Co. 1899

Beers, D.G., *Atlas of Franklin County, Pennsylvania*, B.F. Johnson Publishing, Philadelphia, 1899

Blackford, Charles M., *Letter's from Lee's Army*, Susan Leigh Blackford, Editor, Lynchburg, VA, J.P. Bell Publishing, 1894

Bosse, David, *Civil War Newspaper Maps, (A Historical Atlas)* Johns Hopkins University Press, Baltimore, 1993

Bowman, John S. Editor, *The Civil War Day by Day*, Bronpton Books Corp. Greenwich, CT.,1989

Casdorph, Paul D. *Lee and Jackson*, Dell Publishing Div. of Bantam, Doubleday Dell Publishing, New York, 1992

Clark, George, *A Glance Backward or Some events in the Past History of my Life*, Houston, Privately Publoished, 1914.

Clark, Walter, editor. *Historyies of Several Regiments and Battalions from North Carolina n the Great War 1861-1865 in 5 Vols.* Raliegh,NC, Uzell, 1901

Coddington, Edwin B. *The Gettysburg Campaign, A Study in Command*, New York, Charles Scribner's Sons, 1968

Connelly, Thomas L. *The Marble Man*, New York, Knopf 1977

Bibliography (Cont'd)

Cox, Jacob D. *Military Reminiscences* New York Scribners, 1900

Cresap, Joseph Ord and Cresap, Bernarr, Compilers, *The History of the Cresaps*, The Cresap Society, Macomb, Miss, 1937

Dahlgren, John A., *Memoir of Ulric Dahlgren*, Philadelphia, J.B. Lippincott Publishing, 1872

Davis, Burke, *The Civil War*, Strange and Fascinating Facts, previously published as *Our Incredible Civil War*, New York Holt, Rinehart & Winston 1960 & 1982 Edition New York,Crown Publishers

dePeyster, J. Watts, *Gettysburg and After; Battle of Gettysburg and at Williamsport and Falling Waters*, New York, MacDonald & Co., 1867

Dooley, John E. *Confederate Soldier*, His War Journal, Durkin, James T. Editor, Washigton, Geo. Washington University Press, 1945.

Douglas, Henry Kyd, *I Rode with Stonewall*, Chapel Hill U. of North Carolina Press, 1940

Dowdey, Clifford D.and Manarin, Louis H. Editors, *The Wartime Papers of Robert E. Lee*, Boston, Little Brown & Co., 1961

Dowdey, Clifford Lee, *Lee, with Photos and with Maps by Bryant, Boston, Little*, Brown, 1965

Early, Jubal A. *Autobiographical Sketch and Narrative of the War Between the States*, Philadelphia, 1912

Editor, *The Literary Digest Magazine* New York 1900-1921

Eicher, David J. *Robert E. Lee, A Life Portrait*, Taylor Publishing Co. Dallas, 1997

Faust, Patricia L, Editor, *Encyclopedia of the Civil War*, New York, Harper and Row, 1988

Freeman, Douglas Southall, *R. E. Lee, A Biography*, New York,Charles Scribner's Sons. 1934

Fremantle, Arthur J.L. *The Fremantle Diary or Three Months in the Southern States,(Reprint Edition)* Boston, Little, Brown & Co. 1954

Frye, Dennis E., *2nd Virginia Infantry*, Lynchburg, VA, H.E. Howard, 1984

Gallagher, Gary, Editor, *The Third Day at Gettysburg and Beyond*, University of North Carolina Press, 1994

Gordon, John B., *Reminiscences of the Civil War*, Scribner's, New York, 1904

Gregg, Rod. *Old West Quiz and Fact Book*, Perennial, Harper Row, New York, 1986

Harwell, Richard B. Editor *A Visit to Cities and Camps of the Confederate States, (Reprint Edition)* Chicago, University of Illinois Press, 1958

Henry, J. Maurice, *History of the Church of the Brethren in Maryland*, Brethren, Publishing House, Elgin, Illinois, 1936

Hinman, W.F., *Camp and Field 1861-65* N.G. Hamilton Publishing Co. Cleveland, OH, 1892

Hoke, Jacob, *Great Invasion, The or General Lee in Pennsylvania*, The Otterbein Press, Dayton, OH, 1913

Hood, John B. *Advance and Retreat*, Indiana University Press, Bloomington, 1959

Imboden, John D. *The Confederate Retreat from Gettysburg; Battles and Leaders, Vol 3*

Johnson, R.U. & Buel, C.C., Edited, *Battles and Leaders of the Civil War*, based on The Century Magazine War Series. 1884-

Bibliography (Cont'd)

1887. Thomas Yoseloff, New York. 1956 Kittochtinny Historical Society Papers, papers read before the Society, 1900-1988

Johnston, Joseph E. Narrative of Military Operations, New York, 1872

Jones, J. William; *Personal Reminiscences, Anecdotes and Letters of General Robert E. Lee, New York, 1874*

Jones, John B., *A Rebel War Clerk's Diary*, m Earl Schenk Miers, New York, Sagamore, 1958

Keller, Roger, Ed. *Crossroads of War, Washington County, MD in the Civil War*, Shippensburg, PA; Burd Street Press, 1997

Kidd, James H., *A Cavalryman with Custer*, Hutton, Paul Andrew Bantam Books, New York, 1991 Reprint

Kidd, J.H. *Personal Recollections of a Cavalryman with Custer's Michigan Cavalry Brigade in the Civil War*, Iona, MI, Sentinel Printing, 1908

Krick, Robert E. *Lee's Colonels, A Biographical Register*, Dayton, OH, Morningside Press, 1981

Lake, D.J. *Atlas of Adams County, PA.* Philadelphia, I.W.Field & Co., 1872

Lake, Griffing & Stevenson, *Illustrated Atlas of Washington County*, Maryland, Philadelphia, Lake, Griffing and Stevenson,

Large, George R., *Battle of Gettysburg*, Burd Street Press, Shippensburg, PA, 1999

Lee, Fitzhugh, *General Lee*, D. Appleton & Co, New York, 1894

Lee, Robert E. Captain (Son) *Recollections and Letters of General Robert E. Lee*; New York, Doubleday, 1904

Lee, Susan Pendleton, *Memoirs of W.N. Pendleton*, Philadelphia,

Bibliography (Cont'd)

Lippincott, 1893

Long, A.L. *Memoirs of Robert E. Lee, His military and Personal History Embracing a Large Amount of Information Hitherto Unpublished*, New York, J.M. Stoddard & Co.1886

Longacre, Edward A., *Lee's Cavalrymen*, Mechanicsburg, PA Stackpole, 2002

Longacre, Edward G. *Cavalry at Gettysburg*, Association of University Presses, Fairleigh-Dickinson, N.J.,London,Ontario, 1986

Longstreet, James, *From Manassas to Appomattox, Memoirs of the Civil War in America*, Philadelphia, J.B. Lippincott Co., 1869

Mainwaring, Richard D. MD & Tribble, Curtis G. MD *The Cardiac Illness of General Robert E. Lee*, Surgeon's Library, Department of Surgery, University of Virginia Health Sciences Center, Charlottesville, VA.

Manarin, Louis H and Weymouth, T. Jordan, Jr., Editors *North Carolina Troops 1861-1865, A Roster*, Raliegh,NC North Caolina Division of Archives and History, 1966-89

Marshall, Charles. *An Aide-de-Camp To Lee*, Little Brown Boston, 1927

Maurice, Frederick, Sr. *Robert E. Lee, Soldier*, New York, Hougton Mifflin, Riverside,1925

McClellan, Henry, B., *The Life and Campaigns of Maj-General J.E.B. Stuart Commander of the Cavalry of the Army of Northern Virginia*, Boston, Houghton Mifllin Co. 1885

McCurdy, Charles M. *Gettysburg, A Memoir*, Pittsburgh, Reed & Witting Co., 1929

McKim, Randolph H., *A Soldier's Recollections: Leaves from the*

Bibliography (Cont'd)

Diary of a Young Confederate, New York, Longman's, Green & Co. 1911

Nesbit, Mark, *35 Days to Gettysburg*, Stackpole Books, Mehanicsburg, PA. 1992

Paris, Comte de, *The Battle of Gettysburg*, Porter & Coates, Philadelphia, 1886 Reprinted, Baltimore by Butternut and Blue, 1987

Piston, William Garrett, *Lee's Tarnished Lieutenant*, University of Georgia Press, Athens, Ga. & London, 1987

Porter, John T. *Editor, Under the Maltese Cross, Campaigns of the 156th Pennsylvania Regiment*, Pittsburgh, 1910

Purifoy, John, *The Retreat From Gettysburg*, Confederate Veteran, 1925

Raiford, Neil Hunter, *4th North Carolina in the Civil War*, McFarland and Co., Jefferson, NC, 2003

Robertson, James I, *4th Virginia Infantry*, Lynchburg, VA; H.E. Howard, 1982

Robertson, James I., *Soldiers Blue and Gray*, University of South Carolina Press, 1988

Ross, Fitzgerald, *A Visit to Cities and Camps of the Confederate States*, William Blackwood & Sons, Edinburgh and London, 1865

Royall, William L., *Some Reminiscences*, Neale Publishing, New York, 1909

Savage, Douglas, *The Court Martial of Robert E. Lee, (Fiction)* Warner Books Inc., New York, 1993

Scharf, J. Thomas, *History of Western Maryland*, Philadelphia, Louis H. Everts, 1882

Bibliography (Cont'd)

Shipp, John Simmons, *Holographic Diary, Virginia Historical Society, Battle Abbey, MSS 2, SH646*

Sorrel, G. Moxley, *Recollections of a Confederate Staff Officer*, New York and Washington, D.C. Neasle Publishing 1905

Sorrel, G. Moxley, *Recollections of a Confederate Staff Officer*, New York, Smithmark Publishing,1929

Southern Historical Society Papers, hereafter **SHSP**

Southern Revenge, Greater Chambersburg Chamber of Commerce and White Mane Publishing Co. Inc, Chambersburg, PA, 1989

Stern, Philip Van Doren, Editor, *Robert E. Lee, The Man and the Soldier*, Bonanza Books, New York, 1963

Stoner, Jacob H., Compiled by LuCole Stoner, *Historical Papers of Franklin County and the Cumberland Valley Pennsylvania*, The Craft Press Inc. Chambersburg,1947

Surgery Journal, also; Volume 174, March 1992, pg. 237ff

Swinton, William, *Campaigns of the Army of the Potomac*, New York,Scribner's, 1882

Taylor, John M., *Duty Faithfully Performed. Brassey's*, Dulles, VA, 1999

Taylor, Walter H., *Four Years with General Lee*, New York, D. Appleton and Co., 1877

Trush, Ambrose Wells, MD *Medical Men of Franklin County, (PA)1750-1925*, Medical Society of Franklin County

Tucker, Glenn, *Lee and Longstreet at Gettysburg*, New York, Bobbs Merrill, 1968

U.S. War Department, *The War of the Rebellion*, A Compilation of

Bibliography (Cont'd)

the Official Records of the Union and Confederate Armies, Washington, D.C., US Government Printing Office, 1880-1901. Known hereafter as <u>OR</u>.

Von Borcke, Heros, *Memoirs of the Confederate War for Indepenence*, New York, Smith reprint,1938

Walters, John, Edited by Wiley, Kenneth, Norfolk Blues, *The Civil War Diary of the Norfolk Light Artillery Blues*, Burd Street Press, Shippensburg, 1997

Ward, George W. *History of the 2nd Pennsylvania Veteran Artilllery (1861-1865)*, Philadelphia, Geo. W Ward, 1904

Washington County Free Library, Western Maryland Room, Hagerstown, MD, Vertical File

Whittaker, Frederick A., *A Complete Life of George Armstrong Custer*, University of Nebraska Press. Lincoln, NE and London, 1876, 1993 Reprint

Wittenberg, Eric J., *One of Custer's Wolverines*, Letters of Brig. General James H. Kidd of the 6th Michigan Cavalry.

Wolfe, George "Hooper Wolfe Brochure, Civil War Centennial published by the Mayor and Council of Williamsport, MD. 1962

Articles in Magazines, Periodicals and Collections

Baruch, Simon, <u>Bernard Baruch's father Recounts His Experiences As A Confederate Surgeon</u>, *Civil War Times Illustrated, #4, October 1965*

Battles and Leaders of the Civil War, Johnson, Robert U. & Buel, Clarence C., Editors, New York, Century Co, 1884-1887, 3 Vols

Blackwood's Magazine - Under various published titles, 1817 to 1960?, Edinburgh, William Blackwood, passim

Bradford, Gamaliel, Jr. Atlantic Monthly, 1910-1911; A series of 4 articles on General Lee, His conscience, his spiritual life, his leadership.

Cable, George W., The Gentler Side of Two Great Southerners, Century Magazine, Volume 47, December 1893

Capehart, Henry, <u>Fighting His Way</u>, The Night Passage of Kilpatrick through Monterey Pass, *National Tribune*, January 1895

Confederate Veteran Magazine - Sons of Confederate Veterans. Columbia, TN1995 to present.

Daily Record and Blue Ridge Zephyr, Newspaper, Waynesboro, PA. 1909-1921

Davis, Jefferson, *North American Review, Vol 150, January 1890*

Graves, Charles Marshall, *Recollections of General Lee*, Harper's Weekly, 2 February 1907, Volume 51, #172

Herald, The, Waynesboro, Waynesboro, Franklin Co. PA, 1900

Page, T.N., *Robert E. Lee, Man and Soldier*, North American Review, Vol. 195, March 1912

Parks, Leighton, *A Boy's Recollections of General Lee*, Century Magazine 9 May, 1886, Volume 70, #1

Ranson, A.R.H. *General Lee As I Knew Him*, Harper's Magazine, Vol 122, Feb, 1911

Southern Historical Society Papers, otherwise SHSP, 1st published 1876

United States of America, <u>**OR**</u> *(Official Records) The War of the Rebellion, A compilation of the Official Records of the Union and*

Confederate Armies, Washington, D.C., Government Printing Office, 1880 & following

Valentine, Edward F. *Reminiscences of General Lee*, New Outlook, 22 December, 1906, Volume 84, # ?

Warner, Beers & Co. 1886 *History of Adams County, PA*, Chicago; Warner, Beers and Co, 1886

Williams, Thomas J.C., *History of Washington County, Maryland, from the Earliest Settlements to the Present Times, including a History of Hagerstown, 2 Vols. No Publisher, Runk and Titsworth, 1906*

Index

Index

Index

Index

Index

Index

Index

Index

From Battles & Leaders, Vol. III, by J.P. Longstreet, Lt. Gen. Yoseloff, NY & London, 1956 Reprint, Pg. 250